W9-ANU-785

Cattle Crisis

Scott Wooding

Fitzhenry & Whiteside

Cattle Crisis
Copyright © 2006 Scott Wooding

All rights reserved. No part of this book may be reproduced in any manner without the express written consent of the publisher, except in the case of brief excerpts in critical reviews and articles. All inquiries should be addressed to:

Fitzhenry and Whiteside Limited
195 Allstate Parkway,
Markham, Ontario L3R 4T8

In the United States:
311 Washington Street,
Brighton, Massachusetts 02135

www.fitzhenry.ca   godwit@fitzhenry.ca

Fitzhenry & Whiteside acknowledges with thanks the Canada Council for the Arts, and the Ontario Arts Council for their support of our publishing program. We acknowledge the financial support of the Government of Canada through the Book Publishing Industry Development Program (BPIDP) for our publishing activities.

Canada Council   Conseil des Arts
for the Arts   du Canada

ONTARIO ARTS COUNCIL
CONSEIL DES ARTS DE L'ONTARIO

Library and Archives Canada Cataloguing in Publication
Wooding, Scott
Cattle crisis / Scott Wooding.

ISBN 1-55041-356-2

1. Cattle trade—Canada. 2. Beef industry—Canada. 3. Bovine spongiform encephalopathy—Canada. I. Title.

HD9433.C22W67 2005   338.1'4   C2005-903963-9

United States Cataloging-in-Publication Data

Wooding, Scott.
Cattle crisis / Scott Wooding.—1st ed.
[256] p. : cm.

Summary: An in depth and scientific look at the current crisis stemming from the Mad Cow Disease scare in Canada, the effects on the Canadian beef industry and the trickle down effect felt by farmers, butchers, packers and the buying public.

ISBN 1-55041-356-2
1. Cattle trade—Canada. 2. Beef industry—Canada. 3. Bovine spongiform encephalopathy—Canada. I. Title.
338.1/4 dc22   HD9433.C22W67 2005

Interior design by Darrell McCalla
Cover design by Kerry Plumley
Cover images courtesy of Scott Wooding
Printed and bound in Canada

1 3 5 7 9 10 8 6 4 2

Contents

Preface

I am not a rancher or a farmer, so I have no vested interest in the Canadian cattle industry. But I live and work in the heart of Alberta's cattle country, surrounded by friends and neighbours who are in the business of producing beef, so I do have a strong personal interest in their welfare and in the welfare of our rural communities. When the first case of BSE was confirmed in a cow in northern Alberta on May 20, 2003, the talk everywhere in the area was about what impact the closure of the U.S. border would have on the cattle industry. It didn't take long to find out—the BSE crisis has devastated my friends, neighbours, and everyone else connected to the Canadian cattle industry.

In the midst of the crisis, the idea of writing a book about BSE came up in a discussion with my publisher. I knew something about agriculture and farming from my younger days on my uncle's farm near Chatham, Ontario, where I spent my summers looking after the 40 head of cattle that he backgrounded every year, and from my undergraduate years at the University of Guelph. That I was not an expert in the cattle industry seemed to be a positive factor; although I faced a steep learning curve, I came to the subject with no biases or axes to grind. That allowed me to interview a large number of people in the industry and form my own opinions about the crisis and how it was handled. My findings have been startling. If the Canadian government had been more diligent years earlier, we probably would not have had a case of mad cow disease in Canada. But even worse was how incompetently the government handled the crisis after it hit. BSE exposed serious problems in the cattle industry, especially in export markets and slaughter capacity, and that created the worse crisis the cattle industry has ever faced. It will take many years and some badly needed reforms for the industry to recover. I hope that my outsider's look at the issues will raise awareness and provoke discussion, so that the beef ranchers and farmers of Canada receive the help they deserve in getting their industry back on its feet.

S.W.
Okotoks, Alberta

Acknowledgements

Writing this book would have been impossible for me without a considerable amount of help from many sources. Two people were vital to the development of this book. The first was Bedford Warren who brought me up to date on how today's beef industry works. I owe an even greater debt to the dean of the Canadian beef industry, Charlie Gracey. I am very grateful for the time he took not only to advise me in the writing of this book but in reading the manuscript so carefully.

Many others were also very generous with their time and knowledge, and deserve my heartfelt gratitude. Dave Malinka spent an entire day with me in –30 degree weather. Ian McKillop shared his intimate knowledge of the Ontario farming and ranching community. Probably the most enjoyable day I spent in researching this book was out on the EP Ranch observing the branding of Tom Bews' herd. Tom and his family were very generous with their time and with their knowledge.

Helpful and insightful advice on the relationship between NAFTA and the beef industry was provided by the outspoken and knowledgeable agrologist Wendy Holm.

My thanks also to Ken Yuha, Arno Doerksen, the colorful Cam Ostercamp, Peter Morrison of Roseburn Ranches and the erudite Chris Mills. Dennis Laycraft, of the Canadian Cattlemen's Association and Ted Haney of the Canada Beef Export Federation were very generous with their time and insights into the beef industry.

CHAPTER 1

Mad Cows in Canada

Late January 2003. Marwyn Peaster, a soft-spoken Mennonite running a cow-calf operation near Wanham, Alberta, noticed one of his cows had trouble standing up. The eight-year-old Black Angus had been purchased the summer before at an auction in Lloydminster, Saskatchewan, some 600 kilometres away. The cow, accompanied by its calf, arrived on the Wanham farm along with more than 30 other cow-calf pairs. By January, the Black Angus cow was a "downer," a designation people in the beef industry use to describe animals unable to stand or walk—which indicates serious disease or injury. To prevent the possibility of his cow infecting other animals in the herd—Marwyn Peaster decided to send the cow to slaughter, and on January 31, it was transported to a provincially licensed abattoir, H&M Meats in Grande Prairie.

In Canada, all animals entering abattoirs must be examined by meat inspectors or veterinarians before and after slaughter. The inspector at H&M Meats, who

A Black Angus-Hereford beef herd in the foothills of Alberta

checked the Black Angus cow, suspected it was dying of pneumonia, and condemned the meat as unfit for human consumption. The carcass was sent to a rendering plant to be processed into animal feed. The cow's head was sent to the provincial Animal Health Laboratory in Fairview to be tested for Bovine Spongiform Encephalopathy, or BSE.

Alberta's BSE surveillance program requires inspectors to initiate a post-mortem testing process on all cattle condemned at provincial abattoirs, and this process soon became practice in abattoirs across the country. Health Canada declared BSE a reportable disease in 1990—at the height of the United Kingdom's BSE epidemic—and a Canadian national surveillance procedure was put into place in 1992, wherein meat inspectors and veterinarians targeted for testing all cattle over 30 months of age that were either dead, dying, downers, diseased or showed symptoms that could be a sign of a central nervous system disorder (emaciation, lack of co-ordination, muscle twitching, excessive bellowing, aggressiveness, or "madness").

When the brain of Peaster's Black Angus cow was examined at the Animal Health Laboratory in Fairview, things did not look normal. Scientists removed a piece of the brain stem, and, on February 8, it was forwarded to Edmonton for additional testing by the laboratory run by the Food Safety Division of Alberta's Ministry of

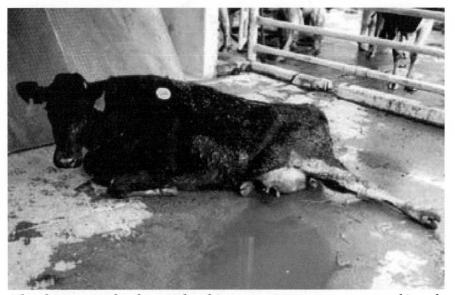

This downer cow has been isolated in a separate pen at a meat packing plant.
Credit: Farm Sanctuary

Agriculture, Food and Rural Development. The tissue sample remained untested at that site for three months.

In February 2003, testing for BSE was not considered a top priority by Canadian food safety officials. All of North America considered itself BSE free. Late in 2002, the Canadian Food Inspection Agency (CFIA) released a report assessing the BSE risk to the country's cattle herd as "negligible." In fact, CFIA, whose job it is to prevent foreign animal diseases from entering the country, was far more worried about foot-and-mouth disease, and cautioned everyone in the livestock industry that a Canadian outbreak of that disease would be a "national disaster."

By May 16, 2003, CFIA priorities changed dramatically when the provincial lab in Edmonton reported the sample from the brain of Peaster's Black Angus cow had tested positive for BSE. The next day the sample was rushed to CFIA's National Centre for Foreign Animal Disease in Winnipeg for confirmation: the results "failed to rule out BSE." Again CFIA rushed brain specimens to the Central Veterinary Laboratory in Weybridge, England, recognized by the World Animal Health Organization, or OIE, as a world reference laboratory for BSE, and on May 20, the British lab verified the first case of BSE in Canada's domestic cattle herd.

Immediately the U.S. closed its border to Canadian beef imports, as did 40 other countries, including Mexico, Japan, South Korea, Taiwan, Australia, China, and Russia.

This was not unusual. It has long been standard practice for trading countries to stop all beef and cattle imports whenever a case of BSE is detected. Canadian officials were not surprised, as they had previously followed the same protocol whenever one of the country's trading partners reported BSE in a domestic herd. No one in Canada, however, was prepared for the impact.

Overnight this country lost more than 60 per cent of its cattle and beef market, most of which had been exported to the United States. Prior to the BSE announcement, in May 2003, Canada shipped almost $5 billion worth of beef products and live cattle across the U.S. border. In 2002, almost 90 per cent of Canadian beef exports and more than 99 per cent of Canadian live cattle exports

---

Canada's Beef and Cattle Trade with the U.S., 2002–2003

In 2002, Canada shipped to the U.S.

- 1.7 million head of live cattle

- 867 billion kilograms (1.091 billion pounds) of beef and veal

In 2003, Canada shipped to the U.S.

- 0.5 million head of live cattle

- 0.335 billion kilograms (0.74 billion pounds) of beef and veal

Source: United States Department of Agriculture (USDA)

---

went to the United States. When the U.S. border closed, the Canadian cattle industry had nothing short of a disaster on its hands.

CFIA failed to keep BSE out of Canada and was forced to manage the crisis. After reassuring Canadian consumers that no parts of Peaster's Black Angus cow had entered the human food system, CFIA officials outlined plans to test all cattle which had been in contact with the cow. "If all those [tests] are negative," the undersecretary of the United States Department of Agriculture announced, "I think we would open the border fairly soon."

However, before such crucial testing could begin, the CFIA had to trace the cow's movements from birth to slaughter. Canada did not have a mandatory identification and tracking system in existence in 1995, the year when the cow was likely born. As a result, CFIA investigators were forced to rely on a combination of DNA testing, information from ranchers, and sales records. That investigation led them initially to Baldwinton, Saskatchewan, and the Black Angus herd of Melvin McCrea. Scientists believed that the BSE cow had probably been born as part of McCrea's herd. Further studies revealed that in the spring of 1998, it was sold and ended up on a farm in Tulliby Lake, Alberta. Still later in that year, the cow moved to Lloydminster, Saskatchewan, to join another cow-calf herd. The Black Angus raised four calves in four years, and all animals went their separate ways. By August 2002, the Black Angus cow was found at a cattle broker, who sold it at auction to Marwyn Peaster.

Peaster's Black Angus cow was a well-seasoned traveler, but the CFIA was able to assume that, somewhere along the line, it had eaten cattle feed containing meat and bone meal (MBM) infected with BSE. The link between BSE and cattle feed produced from carcasses of BSE-infected ruminants had been discovered in 1988 by U.K. scientists, and an immediate ban was placed on the

Tracing BSE

During its BSE epidemic in the 1980s and 1990s, the United Kingdom had established a system of tracking BSE-infected animals, which was based on the Central Veterinary Laboratory's extensive research on how the disease was transmitted. Adopted by other countries reporting the BSE disease in their domestic herds, including Canada, the system involved three lines of investigation:

- **trace back**: tracing the herds and farms where the infected animal had been throughout its life

- **trace forward**: tracing the herds and farms where the infected animal's offspring had ended up

- **feed investigation**: tracing where the rendered products of the infected animal may have been consumed and what feed sources it may have been exposed to during its life

use of rendered ruminant protein in sheep and cattle feed. A similar feed ban was established in Canada, but not until 1997—after the birth of the Black Angus cow. Thus CFIA investigators were forced to track not only those cattle that shared the same farm as the BSE cow, but also any animals which might have eaten the same feed. By May 23, CFIA had issued quarantine orders for nine farms, seven in Alberta and two in Saskatchewan.

CFIA also traced the cow's rendered carcass, which turned up in chicken feed sold in British Columbia. Because cattle on three farms in B.C. used that feed, all three farms were added to the quarantine. CFIA quarantined three more farms in Alberta on May 24, and another location the next day. By May 25 there were 17 farms under quarantine.

Then the slaughter or, as CFIA officials called it, the "depopulation," began. The only true test for BSE was to examine the brains of all suspect animals. Marwyn Peaster's entire herd was eliminated, as was Melvin McCrea's. In total 2,700 cattle were slaughtered and tested, including five bulls linked to the infected cow, but sold in the U.S. in 1997. All animals tested negative for BSE.

Such negative results attest to the singularly strange nature of BSE. How could the disease show up in one cow and not in any of the cattle which had eaten the same feed? The figures were extremely puzzling to health officials, but nevertheless all evidence collected by CFIA pointed to a single and isolated case of BSE.

By the middle of June 2003, CFIA began to wind down its investigation, and invited four international BSE specialists from Switzerland, France, the United States, and New Zealand to review how Canada had handled the investigation of its first homegrown BSE case, and how Canada's BSE policies measured up to international standards.

The experts were impressed and CFIA's final report quoted them: "In a very short time Canadian experts have collected and assessed a level of information that exceeds the investigations done in most other BSE-affected countries." But the experts also had words of caution for Canadian officials and pointed out serious shortcomings in Canada's BSE policies and procedures. On June 26, the same day the report was released, CFIA announced it would introduce new measures immediately to implement the experts' recommendations: including a national ban on Specified Risk Materials (SRMs) in human food; a review of animal feed restrictions; improved tracking and tracing systems; improved disease testing and surveillance; and increased awareness of BSE among producers, veterinarians, and the public.

Federal bureaucrats began working on the recommendations, and the federal Ministry of Agriculture and the Canadian Cattlemen's Association intensified negotiations with the United States and Mexico to reopen Canada's North American beef exports. On September 4, both the U.S. and Mexico announced that they would reopen their borders to boxed beef (boneless, frozen cuts boxed for shipment).

Canadian cattlemen were jubilant. They had reason to hope that within a few months the two borders would also reopen to shipments of live cattle. More good news came on November 4 when the USDA issued a proposal to import bone-in beef and live cattle under 30 months of age. (Most BSE experts consider cattle under 30 months of age to have a very low risk of being infected with BSE.)

On December 23, just as the border seemed poised to reopen, the U.S. reported its first suspected case of BSE in a dairy cow in Washington state. The six-year-old Holstein had been a downer when it arrived at the abattoir on December 9, and that made it an automatic candidate for BSE testing under the USDA's surveillance program. After the cow's brain tested positive at the National Veterinary Services Laboratory in Ames, Iowa, it was sent to the Weybridge laboratory in Britain. A positive result was delivered two days later.

Mexico, Russia, Brazil, Japan, South Korea, and a host of other countries immediately closed their borders to American beef and cattle. Canada imposed a partial ban. In the meantime, the USDA started tracking the life of the diseased Holstein. Shock swept through the Canadian cattle industry on January 6, 2004, when officials from the U.S. and Canada announced that the cow had been born in Alberta in April 1997. Suddenly the spotlight shifted from the U.S. and re-focused on Canada as the home of BSE in North America.

CFIA's investigation into our country's second BSE case was easier and more accurate. The cow had worn an ear tag with a number identifing its herd of origin and CFIA officials traced its movements through herd and registration records. Using farm and feed mill records, CFIA traced the protein supplements and dairy rations the Holstein may have eaten on its birth farm. CFIA investigator's final report, released in March 2004, pointed a finger at BSE-infected meat and bone meal the cow had probably consumed before Canada's feed ban was in place. CFIA traced 12 of the cow's herd mates which had been exposed to the same feed. These animals were slaughtered and tested for BSE. All the results were negative.

The second case of BSE in the country's herd set back Canadian efforts to get live cattle moving across the border. But the picture brightened again on April 18, 2004, when the USDA announced it would lift its restrictions on imports of Canadian ground beef, bone-in cuts, and processed meat from cattle younger than 30 months.

Then suddenly R-CALF USA intervened. The Ranchers-Cattlemen Action Legal Fund, United Stockgrowers of America—an organization of 18,000 independent cattle producers in 47 states, had a mission to protect its members' interests, especially when international trade issues were on the table. Five days after the USDA announced Canadian ground beef would be crossing the border, R-CALF was in a Montana court trying to stop the importation.

R-CALF USA argued that the USDA was breaking its own rules, because one USDA agency, the Animal Health and Plant Health Inspection Service (APHIS), had added a regulation to its books in May 2003 prohibiting imports of ruminants and ruminant meat products from Canada. Although boxed beef had been crossing the border since September 2003 under a USDA escape clause, there would be no escape clause this time around. On April 23, 2004 Judge Richard Cebull, of the U.S. District Court for the District of Montana, granted a preliminary injunction against the importation of Canadian ground beef, bone-in cuts, and processed meat. APHIS immediately withdrew the importation permits it had granted, and Canadian negotiators went back to the drawing board.

Over the next six months, BSE and reopening the border to live Canadian cattle became a political issue in the U.S. presidential election as Republican candidate George Bush and Democratic candidate John Kerry fought for votes in a tight race. Kerry took a tough stance on Canada's BSE problems. Bush needed the support of the right wing of the ranch vote and groups like R-CALF. Candidates in some senatorial races courted voters with the promise of a permanent ban on imports of all Canadian beef and cattle.

President Bush was re-elected in November 2004. On December 1, Bush was in Canada talking to Prime Minister Paul Martin, and before leaving Ottawa, the President announced that in a few months the U.S. border would be again open to live Canadian cattle under 30 months of age. On December 29, the USDA gave Canadian cattle producers a firm date—March 7, 2005.

However, with incredibly bad timing, a new case of BSE turned up in Alberta on December 30. This time it was a 10-year-old dairy cow from a farm near Barrhead. Allan Degner had owned the cow since 1999, and when it started to look like a downer, he asked a vet to euthanize the animal. As CFIA started investigating the case, Agriculture Minister Andy Mitchell told cattle producers on January 4, 2005, that "Canada has been assured by the United States Department of Agriculture that the case will have no impact on the restoration of live cattle and broadened beef trade."

A week later, there was another case. This one was a purebred Charolais beef cow, born on Wilhelm Vohs's ranch near Innisfail, Alberta, in March 1998. The cow had injured itself and was put down by a veterinarian, who sent its brain to a provincial lab for testing. CFIA traced the cow's offspring, and all cattle born on the Vohs's farm 12 months before and after the cow's birth date. It ordered all 41 animals euthanized for testing. All tests were negative.

CFIA focused on what the cow had eaten after birth, and began investigating a calf ration, creep feed, plus two mineral supplements Vohs had purchased for his calves in the spring of 1998—five months after Canada banned ruminant protein in cattle feed. This was not good news for CFIA. It meant either that in March 1998 the feed mill had ignored CFIA regulations and was selling calf rations made before the ban, or that the rations had been contaminated after the ban during the manufacturing process. Neither scenario could be confirmed, but CFIA was forced to conclude that contaminated feed had slipped through the cracks of its feed ban regulations: "The feed manufacturers were handling ruminant MBM for the manufacture of non-ruminant feeds. These feed sources were likely manufactured a short time after the feed ban was implemented; however, as historical production records were not available, manufacturing dates could not be confirmed."

The news was devastating for Wilhelm Vohs. He had complied with all CFIA regulations. And like all purebred stock producers, he had been very careful in how his animals were raised. BSE had still shown up in his herd. Vohs was in the business of raising top-of-the-line purebred Charolais cows and bulls to sell to ranchers wanting to improve their herds. The discovery of BSE in his herd meant very few if any ranchers would buy his stock.

CFIA, however, was more worried about what effect this third Canadian case of BSE would have on the USDA's plans to open the border to live Canadian cattle on March 7. In its report on the investigation, CFIA attempted to forestall criticism from both sides of the border: "This investigation identified that certain feed materials, likely manufactured a short time after the implementation of Canada's feed ban, may have been contaminated. This finding is consistent with the experience of all countries with BSE which have implemented feed bans. As with any major policy that requires restructuring of operations, some time may have been required for the feed ban to be implemented completely and uniformly." The USDA sent animal health experts to verify that the Canadian feed ban was now working effectively. The experts appeared to be satisfied with Canada's regulatory system. As the March 7 reopening date approached, ranchers began to believe that perhaps the 19-month crisis would soon be over.

Then R-CALF and Judge Richard Cebull struck again. On March 2, 2005, Cebull granted R-CALF a temporary injunction, preventing the USDA from reopening the border. He set a date of July 27, 2005 for his ruling on a permanent injunction. It now became very clear to Canadian cattle producers that they were fighting a new and different battle against the interests of American protectionists.

CHAPTER 2

The U.K. Connection

T he Black Angus cow from Marwyn Peaster's farm in northern Alberta was the first case of BSE in Canada's domestic cattle herd. But an earlier case had turned up in 1993 in a cow imported from the U.K. The cow arrived at a farm in Red Deer, Alberta, in January 1987—about the same time that scientists at Britain's Central Veterinary Laboratory in Weybridge were starting to see a new degenerative brain disease in the country's cattle herds. Six years later, the new disease had a name—Bovine Spongiform Encephalopathy—and the U.K. had an epidemic on its hands. By 1993, some 100,000 cattle in the U.K. had tested positive for BSE.

The Red Deer cow was among 182 cattle imported from the U.K. between 1982 and 1990, the year Canada closed its border to cattle imports from countries reporting cases of BSE. With an imported case of BSE in Alberta, Canada's Ministry of Agriculture began tracing all U.K. cattle that had entered the country between 1982 and 1990, as well as their offspring and herd mates. Those cattle that were found alive—a total of 363 animals— were destroyed. Ministry officials discovered that 68 of the original imports had been slaughtered. They also discovered that a few of these animals had been from British herds with at least one case of BSE, and that parts of their carcasses had likely been rendered into feed for cattle and other animals.

Like the rest of the world, Canada was obviously paying attention to the BSE situation in the U.K. Canadian officials had already taken a number of steps to keep BSE out of the country: a ban on imported cattle in 1990, followed

Number of reported cases of BSE in Europe, outside the U.K., by year of confirmation

Country	To 1988	1989	1990	1991	1992	1993	1994	1995	1996	1997	1998	1999
Belgium	0	0	0	0	0	0	0	0	0	0	0	0
France	0	0	0	5	0	1	4	3	12	6	18	31(b)
Ireland (Rep.)	0	15(b)	14(b)	17(b)	18(b)	16	19(b)	16(b)	73	80	83	91
Liechtenstein	0	0	0	0	0	0	0	0	0	0	2	n/a
Luxembourg	0	0	0	0	0	0	0	0	0	1	0	0
Netherlande	0	0	0	0	0	0	0	0	0	2	2	2
Portugal	0	0	1(a)	1(a)	1(a)	3(a)	12	14	29	30	106	170
Switzerland	0	0	2	8	15	29	64	68	45	38	14	50

(a)   Imported cases
(b)   Includes imported cases:
      Republic of Ireland: 5 in 1989, 1 in 1990, 2 in 1991 and 1992, 1 in 1994 and 1995
      France: 1 in 1999
n/a   not available

Source: The BSE Inquiry: *Report, volume 16, chapter 3, figure 3.35.*

in 1991 with a ban on beef from other European countries reporting cases of BSE. By then, Ireland had 46 cases, France had 5, Portugal had 2, and Switzerland had 10, and at least half of these cases were in cattle imported from the U.K. In 1992, Canada instituted a national BSE surveillance program, which established a baseline for BSE testing on cattle most at risk for the disease.

Canada's response to the Red Deer case in 1993 followed the U.K.'s BSE protocol of slaughtering the herd mates and offspring, and that seemed to reassure the country's beef-importing neighbours in North America— the U.S. and Mexico. U.S. investigators sent to Canada to monitor how the country handled the case came away apparently convinced that everything possible had been done to eliminate the risk of BSE establising a foothold on the continent. And with that news, Mexico immediately lifted its temporary ban on beef imports from Canada.

And so Canada picked up where it had left off before the Red Deer case appeared—touting its status as a country free of the disease. And perhaps Canada became a bit complacent, assuming that our import bans and surveillance programs were sufficient safeguards. Somewhere along the way Canadian officials seemed to have missed— or chose to ignore—what turned out to be the most important piece of the BSE puzzle in Britain: the link researchers made in 1988 between BSE and cattle feed produced from rendered ruminant carcasses. All the while, BSE was building up in Canada's cattle herd as dairy and beef calves consumed protein supplements made from carcasses of imported cattle infected with BSE in the U.K.

◆◆◆◆◆

BSE may well have been building in the U.K.'s cattle herds since the 1970s. It was probably showing up sporadically in random cattle in southern England, but for farmers and veterinarians, there was nothing especially mysterious about the symptoms: behavioural changes such as nervousness or aggression; abnormal posture; lack of co-ordination; difficulty in rising or walking; decreased milk production; and weight loss. These same symptoms could be attributed to a number of other cattle problems, such as rabies, parasites, listeriosis, lead and pesticide poisoning. When the animals died or were unable to stand, they went the route of all deadstock and downers—to rendering plants for processing into animal feed and other products.

That was the situation until 1985 when Cow 142 on Pitsham Farm in Sussex became a downer. Seven other cows on Pitsham Farm had developed the same symptoms and died that year. Both Peter Stent, the farmer, and David Bee, his veterinarian, were alarmed and decided to send Cow 142 to the Central Veterinary Laboratory for a post-mortem examination. In their report, pathologists at the lab identified a degeneration in the cow's brain tissue, noting that there were microscopic holes, called vacuoles, which gave the cow brain a spongy appearance, not unlike brains in sheep infected with scrapie.

Another farmer and another veterinarian in southern England were also becoming alarmed at the number of cattle getting sick and dying. On Plurenden Manor Farm in Kent, a county adjacent to Sussex, seven cows and a bull—all showing similar symptoms—had become downers or had died in the past two years. At the end of December 1986, the lab in Weybridge had received three cows for post-mortem from Plurenden Manor Farm, and all showed the same degeneration of brain tissue. By May 1987 the disease had been confirmed in four herds in southern England.

The sudden appearance of the same disease in different herds indicated that it was being transmitted in some way. By the end of December 1987, it appeared to be highly transmissible: there were 370 suspected cases, with 132 confirmed cases clustered on 113 farms, mostly in the south of England. The Central Veterinary Laboratory called the disease Bovine (cattle) Spongiform (spongy) Encephalopathy (brain disease). That classified it as a new form of Transmissible Spongiform Encephalopathy (TSE), the same class of brain disease as scrapie in sheep.

Transmissible Spongiform Encephalopathy in Animals

Scrapie has been showing up in British sheep and goats for 250 years, dating back to 1732. The disease got its name from one of its most characteristic symptoms: sheep with the disease typically rub or scrape themselves against walls and fences, leaving big bare patches in their fleece. Many animals also develop a strange gait, called "trotting," and become noticeably more excitable or nervous. Most sheep die of scrapie about three or four months after initial symptoms appear.

When formal studies of scrapie began in 1913, research-ers noted the following characteristics: vacuoles in the brain's grey matter, producing a spongy appearance; loss of nerve cells in the brain; the spread of astrocytes (small, star-shaped cells surrounding and supporting nerve cells) into damaged tissue; and the presence of a hard, waxy deposit made up of protein and polysaccharides (complex sugars like starch), called amyloid plaque. To date 22 different strains of scrapie have been identified.

Researchers discovered that scrapie can be transmitted by infected material being injected directly into the brain, or by oral ingestion. No one has determined yet exactly what infected material in sheep feed causes scrapie symptoms to appear, despite the efforts of many researchers around the world. This testifies to the complexity of TSE.

In 1965, Transmissible Mink Encephalopathy (TME) was identified on mink farms in Wisconsin. Investigations showed that this too was a highly sporadic disease, affecting only indi-vidual animals rather than entire farms. The brains of TME-infected mink showed damage similar to the brains of scrapie-infected sheep. Very few of the infected mink had been exposed to sheep, so an interspecies transmission—from sheep to mink—was ruled out. Researchers concluded that the infections originated in what the mink were fed, either from commercially prepared rations or from birth materials such as the placenta, which young animals often eat. They also speculated that the disease might have been transmitted through beef and horsemeat that some of the infected mink had consumed.

A few years later another TSE strain was discovered, this time in deer and elk. Called Chronic Wasting Disease (CWD), this form first appeared in 1980 in animals that died in wildlife parks in Colorado and Wyoming. Once again researchers noted extensive brain damage similar to other forms of TSE. Even the family pet has not escaped the TSE class of diseases. A post-mortem on a Siamese cat in Britain in 1990 reported the first case of Feline Spongiform Encephalopathy.

In 1985, there was only one qualified epidemiologist in Britain's Central Veterinary Laboratory. His name was John Wilesmith, and it became his job to find out how and why BSE was transmitted through British cattle herds. After visiting all the infected farms and questioning the herd owners, Wilesmith ruled out transmission by vaccines, hormones, and pesticides, since the disease turned up in cattle not exposed to any of these possible agents.

When Wilesmith and his colleagues investigated what the BSE-infected cattle had been fed, they discovered a common link. All the animals had eaten a protein supplement made from meat and bone meal (MBM) manufactured from rendered animal carcasses. By December 1987, Wilesmith had concluded that the most likely source of transmission of BSE was cattle protein supplements made from meat and bone meal that contained scrapie-infected sheep.

Several things pointed Wilesmith in that direction. Scrapie was endemic to the U.K. sheep population, and the sheep population had been rising since 1980. That meant more scrapie-infected animals were being rendered into MBM. In addition, a significant feature of the rendering process had changed. Previously, the last bits of fat were removed from cooked carcasses by soaking them in a solvent similar to dry-cleaning fluid, then boiling the liquid off. Modern methods used pressure to squeeze the fat out. This change made the rendering business cheaper and more efficient, but Wilesmith believed that, somehow, the scrapie agent was surviving the new rendering process, crossing the species barrier, and causing a new TSE disease in cattle. Wilesmith's conclusions ultimately proved to be wrong, but his theory did lead to measures that finally stopped the spread of BSE.

In May 1988, as a result of Wilesmith's work, the British government established the Southwood Committee to investigate BSE. By June 1988, BSE had become a reportable disease in the U.K., and one month later, the government banned the use of MBM made from ruminants (cattle, sheep, goats, and deer) in all ruminant feed products. To prevent cross-contamination in the rendering process, the ban was extended a few months later to include all animal protein.

Meat and Bone Meal

Since the 1920s, farmers in the U.K. had been feeding their cattle meat and bone meal (MBM) supplements mostly to pregnant cows, newly weaned dairy calves, and older beef calves being "finished," or fattened up for market. The bone meal added calcium and other trace minerals to the feed; the meat meal added protein.

MBM supplements were manufactured by a process called rendering. The bulk of the material that went into the rendering process before the BSE crisis came from waste products from meat packing plants—cattle, pig, and chicken parts that could not be made into food. These parts included bladders, diaphragms, udders, some intestines, kidneys, spleens, blood, stomachs, hearts, livers, and lungs, as well as heads, hooves, bones, and tails. Renderers also accepted downer animals, dead horses, and cattle, sheep, chickens, and family pets that had died from disease or old age. These carcasses, along with rotten meat from grocers and used grease from restaurants, make up about 10 per cent of rendered material.

Rendering is a messy, smelly process that involves crushing the raw materials into small pieces, heating them to temperatures of up to 135°C, draining them to remove the fats, and then pressing the remaining solid material to remove more fat.

The final product, called "greaves" in the U.K. and "cracklings" in the U.S., was sent to animal feed manufacturers where it was mixed with fish meal and wheat meal and made into dry powder or pellets. Farmers usually mixed the MBM powder or pellets with their cattle's hay to increase its protein and mineral content.

MBM was not the only product manufactured from rendered animal carcasses. Others included lubricants, soap, cement, ink, crayons, cosmetics, pharmaceuticals, the majority of gummy candies, gelatin, pet food, lard, glues, and adhesives.

Once it was established that the BSE agent could be transmitted to cattle through feed, some researchers became concerned that infected food could transmit a form of the disease to humans—despite the fact that no Transmissible Spongiform Encephalopathies had ever been known to pass from animals to humans. If BSE could cross the species barrier from cattle to people, experts thought it would probably show up as Creutzfeld-Jakob Disease (CJD), a human TSE whose symptoms and pathology most closely resembled scrapie and BSE. As a precautionary measure, in November 1989, the British government banned Specified Bovine Offal (SBO) from human food. The ban included bovine brain, spinal cord, spleen, thymus, tonsils, and intestines—all the cattle parts, or offal, thought to carry the BSE infection. A few months later, the British government established a CJD surveillance unit to monitor cases of CJD and the possible transmission of BSE to humans.

By 1990, when the CJD surveillance unit was set up, the most common form of the disease was called sporadic CJD, indicating that it appeared spontaneously with no known cause of transmission. Identified as the first human Transmissible Spongiform Encephalopathy in the early 1920s, Creutzfeld-Jakob Disease affected only people of middle age and older. Like all forms of TSE, CJD was invariably fatal. Symptoms included memory loss, mental confusion (and eventually dementia); co-ordination problems and involuntary movements; blindness and loss of speech. CJD has a very long incubation period, up to 15 years, before the onset of symptoms, although once the symptoms do appear, death usually follows within 6 to 12 months. In 1990, worldwide incidence of sporadic CJD was about one case for every million people.

In 1992, the CJD surveillance unit investigated its first case of CJD in a 60-year-old farmer from the Manchester area. The unit concluded that this was a sporadic case of CJD with no link to BSE. In 1993, the unit reached the same conclusion after the death of a 64-year-old farmer from the west of England who had had two BSE-infected cattle in his herd. By then the media had noted these "coincidences" and were on the alert for any new cases of CJD in farmers with BSE in their herds.

The next case, in January 1994, perplexed the experts. A 16-year-old girl died after showing symptoms very close to CJD. She had not lived on a farm or been exposed to cattle with BSE. And then in December that year, another farmer, whose herd had BSE, died from CJD. This time, members of the surveillance unit were forced to admit that there was little chance that this fatality was a coincidence. They did not, however, make any public announcement or recommend any new health safety measures, assuming that the 1989 ban on Specified Bovine Offal in human food was sufficient.

In May 1995, two more fatal cases of CJD were found in teenagers, and by the end of the year, the surveillance unit was investigating 10 more CJD deaths— all in people under the age of 50. On March 20, 1996, came the news no one wanted to hear: the appearance of a new form of CJD linked to BSE. "Although there is no direct evidence of a link," the government reported, "on current data and in the absence of any credible alternative, the most likely explanation at present is that these cases are linked to exposure to BSE before the introduction of the Specified Bovine Offal ban in 1989. This is cause for great concern."

The new form of CJD was called variant Creutzfeld-Jakob Disease (vCJD). The differences between this new form and those strains previously identified included the younger age of those in which the symptoms began to appear (median age for vCJD was 29 as apposed to 66 for other forms); the clinical symptoms; the pattern of brain waves; and the pathology or nature of the lesions and plaques formed in the brain.

Creutzfeld-Jakob Disease

Three distinct forms of CJD have been identified to date. The first, which makes up between 85 and 90 per cent of CJD cases, is a sporadic form which appears spontaneously with no known cause of transmission. The second form shows up in less than 10 per cent of cases, and is inherited from a parent through a dominant gene. The third human form of CJD, which occurs in about 1 per cent of all CJD cases, is acquired through medical procedures in which neural tissues from an undiagnosed CJD patient end up infecting another patient.

A much rarer form of a human TSE, Gerstman-Straussler-Scheinker Disease, was discovered in Germany in 1928. This disease has both inherited and sporadic origins, but differs slightly from CJD in its symptoms, which are primarily disturbances in speech and movement. Once these symptoms appear, the patient may survive for about five years. This strain's incidence is 2 to 5 cases per 100 million people.

Still another human TSE has shown up only in the South Fore people of Papua, New Guinea. The disease, called Kuru, which means trembling in the local language, was discovered in 1957. Very similar to CJD, it was found to be transmitted through a funeral ritual in which the brain and internal organs were consumed by relatives, mostly women and children, as a sign of respect. Typical of TSEs, only a fraction of those participating in the ritual—about 1 per cent of the South Fore population—actually contracted Kuru. Researchers believe that it may have originated from a single case of sporadic CJD that appeared early in the twentieth century.

Finally, a relatively new form of human TSE, called Fatal Familial Insomnia, was discovered in 1986. Symptoms include progressive insomnia and problems in the autonomic nervous system, which controls functions of the body's internal organs. Death usually occurs within nine months of symptom onset.

Transmissible Spongiform Encephalopathies

TSE	Host
Scrapie	Sheep, Goats
Transmissible Mink Encephalopathy	Mink
Chronic Wasting Disease	Mule Deer, Elk
Feline Spongiform Ecephalopathy	Cats
Bovine Spongiform Encephalopathy	Cattle
Creutzfeld-Jakob Disease	Humans
Gerstman-Straussler-Scheinker Disease	Humans
Kuru	Humans
Fatal Familial Insomnia	Humans

The circumstantial link between BSE and vCJD—the fact that the two were associated both in time and space, and almost exclusively in the U.K.—was quickly verified by experimental and biochemical results. The next step was to figure out how the disease was transmitted from cattle to humans. Investigators suspected that people had contracted vCJD before the 1989 ban on Specified Bovine Offal in human food. The transmission source was likely processed meat containing brains, spinal cords, and nerves from cattle infected with BSE.

Number of BSE Cases in the U.K. by Year of Origin

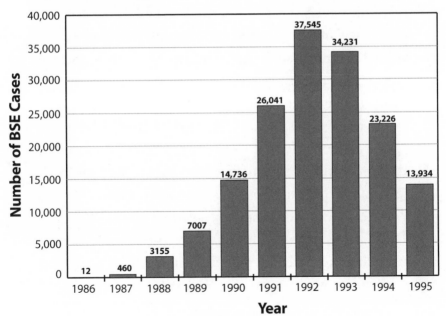

As the news of the BSE-vCJD link became public in 1996, the U.K. was just begining to see the results of its 1988 ban on feeding ruminant-derived meat and bone meal back to ruminants. The number of cases of BSE in British was declining, from a peak of more than 37,500 cases in 1992 to less than 14,000 in 1995. Government officials were predicting the same pattern for vCJD—an increase in cases because of the long incubation period followed by a decline. But they were forced by media outrage and consumer panic to take drastic measures. In April 1996, the British government ordered the slaughter of all cattle over 30 months of age. Some 4.5 million cattle were destroyed.

With the BSE-vCJD link firmly established, there was now a new urgency to find the cause of both human and animal transmissible spongiform encephalopathies. Researchers studying scrapie had determined by the 1950s that neither bacteria nor virus caused the disease. In the early 1980s, Stanley Prusiner of the University of California published his theory that TSEs were caused by abnormal misfolded proteins, which he called proteinaceous infective particles, or prions for short. Though Prusiner's prion idea did not solve all the mysteries of TSEs, it has become the most accepted theory among researchers to date. In 1997 Prusiner received a Nobel prize for his work on prions and TSEs.

BSE destroyed the U.K.'s cattle industry. Twenty years after the disease first showed up on farms in southern England, the U.K. is still designated by world animal health organizations as a high-risk country for BSE. And more than 80 countries have kept their borders closed to all cattle and beef from the U.K. Even in the aftermath of hurricane Katrina in 2005, U.S. officials refused to distribute British military rations sent in as relief aid for hurricane victims, because these rations contained British beef.

In 1993 the Canadian cattle industry got off easy, when the first case of BSE showed up in a cow in Red Deer, Alberta. Although Mexico closed its border temporarily, the U.S. kept its border wide open. Because the animal had been imported from the U.K., the BSE infestation was dismissed as a British problem, not a Canadian one. That was Canada's first big mistake. It was obvious a decade later that BSE prions from infected animals imported from the U.K. had been transmitted to Canada's domestic herd through cattle feed.

What We Know About BSE

• BSE can be transmitted through feed containing meat and bone meal manufactured from carcasses of infected cattle.

• The BSE agent did not develop from scrapie, and changes in the rendering process did not affect its transmission.

• According to Stanley Prusiner's theory, BSE and other TSEs are characterized by abnormal proteins that cause nearby normal prions to change their shape to the infectious form.

• It takes only a very small amount of infectious material, possibly as little as 1 gram of brain tissue, to infect an animal.

• BSE may be transmitted to humans in the form of Creutzfeld-Jakob Disease, probably through eating infected specified risk materials (SRM's), such as the brains, spinal cord or ileum of an infected animal.

And What We Don't Know

• The biggest mystery about BSE is why it strikes so randomly, affecting only one or two cows in a herd wherein all the animals have eaten the same feed. Recent research from Switzerland, published in the respected journal *Science*, indicates that the abnormal prions may be transmitted through the urine of infected animals, although considerable research is still necessary to confirm this finding.

• The mechanism by which the prions become abnormal, or misfolded into an infectious shape, is still unknown.

Raising Calves

The discovery of BSE in Canada in 2003 has hurt ranchers, farmers, and everyone else in the country's agricultural industry. But the bulk of the suffering has fallen directly on Canada's 90,000 beef producers, with the hardest blow hitting Alberta ranchers. About 80 per cent of the beef cows in Canada are in the West: Alberta has half of them, Saskatchewan follows with 28 per cent of the country's beef cows, and Manitoba has 12.5 per cent.

Ranchers and farmers in Alberta have been hit by disasters before—snowstorms that wiped out complete herds and thousands of cattle, droughts that wiped out crops and grassland. But the BSE crisis caused far more damage to our cattle industry than any blows dealt by Mother Nature. Today ranchers and farmers are raising animals that have nowhere to go. The loss of its major export market may be the worst disaster in Alberta's ranching history.

Alberta Beef

Between 1999 and 2003, 99 per cent of Alberta's beef exports went to markets in the United States, Mexico, Japan, South Korea, and Taiwan.

In 2002 Alberta's largest customer, the United States, purchased over 80 per cent of the province's total beef exports, worth $1.3 billion.

Mexico has been Alberta's second market, accounting for 14 per cent of the province's total beef exports in 2002.

In 2002 about 5 per cent of Alberta's total beef exports was destined for Japan, Alberta's third largest market.

Since the 1880s, Alberta has been recognized as a perfect place for raising large numbers of cattle. Early ranchers were attracted to the area by the combination of dry climate and open grazing land, where nutritious prairie grasses could support hardy animals through all seasons. Ranchers were also attracted by incentives offered by Sir John A. Macdonald's government, which needed to secure the West for Canada, in addition to justifying expensive plans for a transcontinental railway. A key part of Macdonald's scheme was to develop large ranches in the West that could ship finished beef via the Canadian Pacific Railway to ready markets in the East. As an incentive, his government offered potential ranchers a very generous land-leasing arrangement—100,000 acres for 21 years at one cent per acre per year.

By the time the Canadian Pacific Railway reached Calgary in 1883, corporate investors had set up several large ranches with cattle driven up from Idaho and Montana. The Cochrane Ranche, owned by Senator Matthew Cochrane of Quebec, started with a herd of 3,000 cattle; by 1903 it was raising 13,000 head. Another of the early ranches was the Bar U, established by the North-West Cattle Company. Its principal shareholder was shipping magnate Sir Hugh Allan, who owned the Allan Steamship Line. There was also the E.P. Ranch, situated near the Bar U, not far from Pekisko, Alberta. It was founded by an English widow and her son in 1886, and became famous when it was bought in 1919 by Edward, the Prince of Wales (later King Edward VIII, and after his abdication, Duke of Windsor).

Those were the days of larger-than-life cowboys and round-ups that meant months in the saddle, covering the territory from Calgary all the way to the U.S. border. During the spring round-up, newborn calves were branded, males were castrated, and then left on the open range with the cows to fend for themselves. It usually took four to five years of grazing for animals to reach market weight. Cowboys rounded the animals up in the fall, driving them in herds to the nearest railhead.

The harsh winter of 1886-1887 killed thousands of range cattle and forced some ranches out of business. Twenty years later, entire herds starved to death when heavy snowfalls covered grazing land. For the devastated ranchers, raising huge herds of beef on the open range no longer seemed viable. They were also being hit by the homesteading movement, as more and more settlers took up land grants and began to carve up cattle country. By the first decade of the twentieth century, there were only a few large-scale ranches left in Alberta. Even fewer cattlemen left their animals to fend for themselves. Most started growing or buying hay to feed their cattle through the brutal prairie winters.

Cattlemen have turned out to be a committed lot. They have adapted their way of raising beef more than a few times over the past one hundred years. Today, few cattlemen raise animals from birth to final market weight. The beef industry now has four production sectors: purebred cattle; cow-calf; backgrounder; and feedlot. Most cattlemen end up specializing in the two major sectors, either raising calves in a cow-calf operation, or feeding beef in a feedlot operation.

Beef Production Sectors

Purebred Cattle

This sector of the beef industry raises purebred bulls and breeding heifers for cattlemen who want to improve their herds. Bulls are generally ready to sell when they reach 12 to 18 months of age. Most young heifers are sold to cow-calf operators as replacements for old or unproductive cows. Purebreds that don't make the cut for quality are marketed as commercial feeder cattle.

Cow-Calf Operation

The production of beef begins at a cow-calf operation where a herd of breeding cows is maintained in order to produce an annual crop of calves. Cows are selected for their breeding and mothering ability—that means dropping a calf each spring and nursing it to a weaning weight of about 225 to 270 kilograms (500 to 600 pounds) by the fall.

On most operations, the cows and their calves spend all their time on pasture and grassland. When weaned at six to eight months of age, the calves either are sold to feedlots for finishing or are over-wintered in a backgrounding operation.

A cow-calf operation of crossbred Black Angus and Hereford

Backgrounding

Backgrounding involves feeding weaned calves over the winter until they reach a weight of about 400 kilograms (900 pounds). Most are fed a hay-based diet in winter shelters. Some cow-calf operators over-winter their own calves until they're heavy enough to sell to a feedlot.

The Feedlot

In a feedlot, calves are finished, or brought up to market weight, about 500 to 550 kilograms (1,100 to 1,200 pounds). In this intensive part of the production process, the animals are kept in a confined area dominated by feed bunks. They receive a high-grain ration for 60 to 120 days, which produces the tender, marbled beef favoured by consumers.

For all cow-calf operators, there is a yearly cycle that turns on breeding and calving. On Alberta ranches, most calves are born from late February to early April. That gives them six to seven months to put on weight before the fall sales start. Calves that gain weight quickly, or heavy calves, are usually ready for a feedlot or auction as early as the end of September.

Some cow-calf operations have moved to calving in the late spring and early summer. These calves tend to be smaller, which makes for easier deliveries and fewer assisted births. Summer calves gain weight more quickly and, while they are not as heavy at weaning as the winter calves born in late winter and early spring, they are close.

A few days after the calving season (usually in three to five weeks depending on the size of the herd) is over, the newborn calves are branded, tagged, dehorned if necessary, and vaccinated for such endemic diseases as black leg and malignant edema. Branding newborn calves has gone the way of most symbols of the old west. First came ear tags with bar codes (introduced January 1, 2001 and made mandatory for all Canadian cattle on July 1, 2002), but these are now being replaced by a new ear-tagging system, which will become mandatory in Canada on September 1, 2006. The new ear tags emit a radio frequency with a unique identifying number that allows animals to be traced from birth to slaughter. The implementation of the new system has been rapidly stepped up as a direct result of the BSE crisis.

Before the cows and their calves are left alone to graze and gain weight, the young males are castrated and most female calves are either spayed or given hormones to prevent them from cycling. The best heifers are kept as replacements for older cows in the herd that have reached the end of their breeding life, generally around 10 years of age. In earlier times, ranchers replaced 10 to 15 per cent of their breeding cows each year. That was in the pre-BSE days when there was a market for cull cows.

To keep the cycle moving, ranchers put the bulls in with the cows in April for a spring calving, and in August for a summer calving. At the end of a perfect breeding season, each cow is pregnant and has a nursing calf—"one on them and one in them." Many ranchers have their cows "preg-tested" shortly after the end of the breeding period, which usually lasts for 60 to 65 days. Pregnancy testing happens at the same time that the calves from the last breeding are weaned, a process which ideally starts when they are six months of age and weighing in at 250 kilograms (550 pounds). That means that calves born in late April are usually weaned by the end of October.

A calf that attains a high weaning weight in six months is the sign of a good cow and good genetics. Most ranchers and farmers in Alberta want cows that deliver small calves with ease and calves that make a rapid weight gain. In Alberta, that usually means cattlemen

Gelbvieh cow and calf

stocking their beef cow herds with crossbreds from a number of preferred breeds: Black and Red Angus, Hereford, Gelbvieh, Simmental (or Fleckvieh), Charolais, and Saler.

At weaning, some of the heavier calves, weighing between 250 to 315 kilograms (570 to 700 pounds), are immediately sold to feedlots. Mid-size calves, weighing 225 to 270 kilograms (500 to 600 pounds), are either kept in the herd until they reach the heavier weight, or sold to backgrounders who fatten them up for the feedlot. The smaller calves, weighing 160 to 270 kilograms (350 to 500 pounds), along with those born later in the season, are kept over the winter until they reach 360 kilograms (800 pounds). Often called "long yearlings," these calves will be about 18 months old by the time they are sold for finishing, either through a cattle auction or directly to a feedlot. A good finished weight is about 540 kilograms (about 1,200 pounds).

The major source of ranching income comes from the sale of weaned calves. Before the BSE crisis, the sale of culled cows and bulls was considered "gravy." When a cull cow was going for about $800, ranchers selling old and unproductive animals from large herds of 300 breeding cows could add $24,000 to $36,000 a year to their income. Those were the days when the sale of culled animals accounted for about 17 per cent of the annual income of an average cow-calf operation.

Post-BSE, the price for a culled animal dropped to $200 or less, and many farmers, hoping for a better market and an open border, decided to hold on to their cull cows and feed them through the winter. A recent Saskatchewan study has shown that keeping one beef animal for a year costs between $470 and $660—a considerable amount for ranchers to pay out when they are already strapped for cash. A lack of slaughter capacity for cull cows has made matters even worse.

Backed into a corner by the lack of markets and slaughter capacity for cull cows, many ranchers followed the old philosophy that "if you keep her, you might as well breed her." The result has been a big growth in Canada's beef cow herd, from 4.9 million in July 2003 to about 5.3 million in January 2005. For ranchers, that comes as more bad news. Before the BSE crisis, many experts in the cattle industry were already saying that Canada's cow herd was getting too large.

Consuming Canadian Beef

At best, Canadians have consumed only about 40 per cent of the country's beef production, which includes beef from steers and heifers as well as from the culled cows and bulls. Before BSE closed borders to Canadian cattle and beef in May 2003, the rest of the production was destined for export, mostly to the United States.

The cost of feed has become a very critical factor in these lean times for beef producers. Ranchers have watched their fixed costs of growing feed—fertilizer, pesticides and herbicides, fuel, equipment expenses, for example—continue to rise as cattle prices have dropped to record lows.

Ranchers who have been able to maintain their cows and raise their calves on natural grasses have fared better than most producers. Many Alberta farmers consider that each cow-calf pair needs about 1.6 hectares (four acres) of good grassland. When there is not enough grass, or when its quality is low, ranchers often turn to feeding hay.

Hay is relatively cheap to produce, and costs in the West range from $25 to $50 per acre. When ranchers buy hay, they face prices between $50 and $100 a ton. In the early fall of 2004, Saskatchewan hay prices were between $75 and $85 per ton; later in the fall, they fell to a range between $55 and $65. A cow weighing 500 kilograms (1,100 pounds) requires an average of 2 per cent of its body weight of hay per day (about 10 kilograms, or 22 pounds), and twice that much in very cold weather. For a herd of 300 cattle, that means feeding a minimum of 3 tonnes (3.3 tons) of hay daily.

Another cattle feed alternative is silage, which is made from grass, legumes, or cereals (such as wheat, barley, corn) allowed to ferment. Silage can be harvested in almost all weather conditions with a minimum loss of nutrients, and packs more nutrients per acre, but it also requires considerable labour as well as special equipment. According to Manitoba's Department of Agriculture, the cost of feeding silage is about 33 per cent higher than the cost of feeding hay alone.

When hay is in short supply, some farmers turn their cereal crops into green feed for their cattle. Wheat, oats, and barley are cut before the grain ripens and then baled like hay. Generally, these crops are used as green feed only when the quality is too low to sell as grain or when grain prices are too low.

◆◆◆◆◆

Tom Bews considers himself lucky. He raises his calves on natural prairie grasses, supplementing with hay or silage only when winters are especially harsh. His cow-calf operation is a classic example of a large-scale Alberta ranch.

A former Canadian All-Around Rodeo Champion, member of the Canadian Rodeo Cowboy Hall of Fame, and movie wrangler, who once doubled for Burt Reynolds, Tom Bews owns a spread that is right out of a Hollywood film. Between his own property and the land he operates in partnership with Curtis Bartlett, Tom runs around 1,000 cattle in about 30 sections (7,770 hectares, or 19,200 acres) of land, not including the 10 sections of forestry reserve land that he leases. His ranch, called the Big Loop Cattle Company, is nestled in the foothills of the Rocky Mountains along the Highwood River. His family has owned a ranch here since the notorious winter of 1906 when thousands of cattle starved to death. While the original family property, the Sullivan Ranch, has been split between Tom and his two brothers, Tom's Big Loop portion has been increased many times by the acquisition of both the Cartwright Ranch and the E.P. Ranch, once owned by the Prince of Wales.

Most of Tom's 1,000 head of cattle, which includes bulls, cows, and calves, are either Hereford or Black Angus crosses. Tom breeds about 150 of the heifers and second-year cows to Saler bulls. The Saler is a French breed noted for its ability to forage on native grasses. Growing hay and grain to feed his cattle isn't an option on Tom Bews's ranch. The soil is too rocky and the altitude—above 1,200 metres (4,000 feet)—is too high.

Just like in the old west though, everything possible on Tom's ranch is done on horseback. The family saddles up at the end of February to drive all the cows from their winter range to about two and a half sections of the E.P. ranch near Pekisko. Protein pellets, the only type of feed purchased for the Big Loop's cattle, are spread in the grass to build up the cows before calving begins in mid-April.

During calving season, Tom and his youngest son, Peter, cover about 45 kilometres (30 miles) each day on horseback to check the cows and newborn calves. In 2004 they lost only about 3 per cent of the calves from 550 cows, which made it an excellent calving season. Before the end of May, the cow-calf pairs are moved to the former Cartwright ranch. Here, around the middle of June,

Roping cattle at branding time, Tom Bews ranch

the new calves are branded, tagged, castrated, and vaccinated—a job that takes just one day but involves about 30
people. The calves get five or six days to recover, and then
cows and calves are split into two herds, one predomi-
nantly Black Angus and the other mainly Hereford. In
2005, creeks in the area flooded badly and washed out
two major culverts, making it impossible for Tom to move
his herds. The branding, tagging, and vaccinating had to
be delayed by two weeks.

At the end of June, the two herds are moved to the
high country for summer pasturing. This area is deep in
the foothills of the Rockies, at around 1,500 metres
(5,000 feet), in what is known as Kananaskis Country.

Each cowboy on the cattle drive takes four horses, including a young one that needs breaking in. Four pack mules and a mule team pull a buckboard to carry supplies to a temporary "cow camp" from where Tom and his cowboys move the animals as high as possible. The bulls are sent out around the first of July. In 2004, Tom ended up with about 7 per cent open, or dry, cows, which he kept to try to breed the following spring. This decision was a direct result of the BSE crisis since there is virtually no market for cull cattle.

For three days a week through July, August, and September, Tom and his crew are out with the cattle, keeping them in the high country and away from the creek bottoms, and replacing their salt licks. In mid-September, it's time to move the cattle to their fall pasture at the old Cartwright Ranch. By then, the herd is scattered all over the rolling foothills. But Tom's animals are smart. Before the round-up gets into full swing, the cattle start to come down on their own. Gates are left open so that any stragglers missed in the round-up can rejoin the herd. Just before Christmas, the cattle are moved to their winter pasture at the old E.P. Ranch. Here the cattle graze on natural grasses all winter long. Then the cycle begins all over again at the end of February when the two herds are combined for calving.

Tom Bews says that the BSE crisis has caused him to "screw down" and become as efficient as possible in raising his calves. Fortunately, his fixed costs are not as high as they are on ranches that have to grow or buy cattle feed. Nevertheless, Tom has had to cut back. Some of his buildings are no longer insured, and older buildings won't be getting repaired or replaced anytime soon. There won't be any new equipment or purchases of large quantities of hay, which Tom likes to have on hand to feed his horses and cattle in case heavy snows cover the pastures during the winter months.

To maintain some cash flow, Tom decided to sell 75 cull cattle. They went for extremely low prices to XL Foods in Calgary, the only major packer that would slaughter them. In better years, Tom has sold twice that number of culls. He has also had to sell off some lighter calves that he would normally have wintered over to increase their weight and add more value to them.

Tom thinks that ranchers can learn some lessons from the BSE crisis, especially how to manage their herds better. Before BSE struck, the beef industry was on a "runaway," he says. With good prices and a ready market for all cattle, many ranchers, particularly the smaller ones, were not paying attention to the quality of their product or following efficient feeding and production practices. Many ranchers in Alberta are already improving their efficiency, and if that continues to grow, Tom feels that the BSE crisis will leave behind at least one positive effect.

With about 1,000 wintered-over cattle, Tom Bews's ranch is huge by Canadian standards. But there's a few of them that come much bigger than this. The Douglas Lake

Ranch, located on 210,000 hectares (about 500,000 acres) south of Kamloops, B.C., winters over 15,000 head of cattle each year, and produces an annual crop of about 6,500 calves. About 80 per cent of Canada's cow-calf operations have fewer than 100 beef cows. Ian MacLachlan, author of *Kill and Chill,* says that ranchers need at least 100 head of cows to make a full-time occupation and generate enough income. Many ranchers facing the BSE crisis think that a more viable operation these days is a mixed one that combines sales from a herd of 100 cows and income from cash crops.

Dave Malinka runs a mixed operation near Vegreville, Alberta. He maintains a herd of 130 beef cows; in 2004 they raised 114 calves. Dave has moved to a summer calving system, so he sends his four bulls out in late August and expects to begin calving in mid-May. In the fall of 2004, he bought 120 calves for backgrounding. The calves averaged 200 kilograms (450 pounds), and Dave's plan was to keep the animals for about 120 days during which he hoped they would gain at least 90 kilograms (200 pounds). The calves were right on target with an average weight gain of .77 kilograms (1.7 pounds) per day. Dave's profit on his backgrounders was about $100 per calf. With the expectation that the U.S. border would reopen on March 7, 2005, beef prices rose, and Dave was able to sell his own calves at relatively good prices, around $1.25 per pound. He also had 50 calves in the government-sponsored Set-Aside Program, which

Set-Aside Program

On September 10, 2004, the Canadian and Alberta governments offered beef producers in the province a voluntary program that offered to pay them $200 a head to delay fattening up some of their calves to slaughter weight. Under the program, calves had to be set-aside for one year. Governments were hoping that the program would keep 40 per cent of the 2004 calf crop out of the slaughter houses, which had no capacity to process them.

paid him $200 for every calf he kept out of the slaughter house and off the market. In the end, Dave came out slightly ahead.

The price of barley is important to Dave Malinka. In order to get his calves to put on weight faster, they are fed grain along with their hay, silage, or green feed. The amount varies with the weight of the calf, but Dave calculates that the backgrounded calves need less than half a kilogram (about 1 pound) of grain, usually barley, for each hundredweight of calf per day. That means that a calf weighing 250 kilograms (500 pounds) needs to consume 2.25 kilograms (5 pounds) of grain each day. In his operation, the total comes to 27 tonnes (30 tons) of barley over the course of 100 days, a cash outlay of $3,600. That cost is on top of what Dave spends on silage and green feed that he feeds them each day. Even if Dave grows the feed himself, it means that he loses the money he would have obtained by selling the grain.

Although Dave's herd is larger than the number recommended for a full-time operation, he does not find 130 beef cows sufficient to make a living, even in good times. To supplement his beef income, Dave also raises canola and barley as cash crops. Most years he has 120 hectares (300 acres) in canola, 100 hectares (250 acres) in barley, and 65 hectares (160 acres) in oats, which he uses for green feed. To make a decent profit selling his canola, he needs the price per bushel to be between $7 and $8. Dave watched anxiously as canola prices hovered around the $6 level for several months. He finally sold his crop for $6.48

Dave Malinka's backgrounder calves eating their daily grain ration

a bushel. With both cattle and grain prices down at the same time, Dave was forced to take a part-time job at a local feedlot, working four hours a day during the winter months.

There was more bad luck waiting for Dave Malinka. One of his bulls died over the winter, forcing him to make a difficult decision. Up to that point, he had submitted animals that had died in his herd to the government-sponsored BSE Surveillance Program, which paid him $225 to have the animal tested by a veterinarian. However, when Dave's bull died just after two new BSE cases were reported in Alberta in January 2005, he was extremely worried about the possibility of "being on Global at noon." In the end, he did the right thing, but his indecision is typical of the reaction of many ranchers and farmers in Alberta when faced with a downer or a dead animal in their herd. With their herd's and their own reputations at stake, some ranchers and farmers might consider following Alberta Premier Ralph Klein's tongue-in-cheek advice to "shoot, shovel, and shut up."

Dave finds it difficult to estimate his total losses from the BSE crisis. The biggest losses came during the months immediately after May 20, 2003, when the U.S. border was totally closed and beef prices hit rock bottom. When the border reopened to boxed beef in August 2003, prices improved a bit but have never returned to pre-crisis levels.

Dave's major problem is the lack of markets for his cull cattle. He held back 15 heifers in 2005 as replacements, but cannot get rid of the older cows. The result is an older herd of breeding cows. The ability of his herd to produce calves remains the same, or increases slightly if the older cows catch and reproduce, but his feed bills continue to mount. The loss of earnings from culled cattle, which used to be a big factor in Dave's ranch income, has been one of the most economically damaging impacts of the BSE crisis across the country.

This is certainly the case for Ian and Alan McKillop who run a mixed farm that includes a cow-calf operation near Dutton, Ontario. The McKillop family has farmed this land since 1851. When their father died in 1970, Ian and Alan, along with their mother and sister, ran the home farm of 60 hectares (150 acres). In 1984 the family bought the farm across the road and then two more. The McKillops now own about 325 hectares (800 acres): 60 hectares (150 acres) in corn, 80 hectares (200 acres) in soybeans, 50 hectares (130 acres) in wheat, and the rest in hay or pasture.

Raising Beef in Ontario

Ontario has the fourth largest cattle herd in the country, following Alberta, Saskatchewan, and Manitoba. There are about 21,000 beef producers in the province. The average number of beef cows in an Ontario cow-calf herd is 23. In Alberta the average number is 63 cows.

Anticipating better times ahead, the McKillop brothers recently doubled the size of their beef cow herd to 140 cows, which now includes 30 heifers from their own calf crop from the previous year and 39 bred heifers purchased from a northern Ontario herd. The herd is mainly Charolais, a well-muscled breed that produces a maximum weight gain, but the McKillops are gradually switching to Red Angus, Simmental, and Gelbvieh cows crossed with Charolais bulls. They are aiming for smaller calves at birth and an improved feed-to-weight-gain ratio.

Pasture grasses and dry hay are the staple food for the cows. Once the calves are weaned, they are fed corn silage through the fall and winter months. Unlike most cow-calf operators, the McKillops finish their own calves, feeding them straight corn for two months before they head to market.

Ian and Alan start selling their finished calves in June, at 15 months of age. When finished, the steers weigh in at 635 kilograms (1,400 pounds) and the heifers at 545 to 590 kilograms (1,200 to 1,300 pounds)—slightly heavier than finished steers and heifers in western Canada.

The McKillops don't have enough grazing land to maintain their cows and raise their calves on grass. That means hefty feed bills for supplementary hay and silage rations. The brothers grow most of their own hay and buy the rest from a neighbour. Overall, the cost of feeding cattle in Ontario is generally higher than in the prairie provinces.

Part of Ian and Alan McKillop's cow herd, which includes Charolais and Red Angus crosses

Ian McKillop estimates that their income from beef is down about 30 per cent since the U.S. border closed in May 2003. Like other ranchers and farmers in the country, the McKillops have lost income because they can't sell their cull cattle. Last year they did not cull any cows from their herd. Since the cows that should have been culled were fetching only about $150 at auction, the McKillops kept them in the hopes that each might produce another calf. Ten of these older cows died, leaving behind zero income. Before BSE hit, they would have sold for a minimum of $700 a head, so, just on these 10 culls, the McKillops lost $7,000 of income. Submitting dead and downer cattle to the BSE Surveillance Program in Ontario brings in only $75 per animal. That's a lot less than the $225 that farmers receive in Alberta, where the province tops up federal funds for BSE testing.

Ken Yuha, a teacher in Okotoks, Alberta, runs a part-time operation, which is the most common type of cow-calf business in Canada. Ken maintains 59 cows, mostly Red Angus or Simmental crosses, on 60 hectares (150 acres) that he owns and another 140 hectares (350 acres) that he rents. About half of the land grows hay and the other half is grazing land. Ken likes his calving season to start in February, a month that for the past 10 years has been relatively mild and dry in Alberta. His three bulls are

Ken Yuha's Gelbvieh bull has just been put out with the cows, which are nursing three-month-old calves.

busy breeding the cows from the end of April to mid-June. Yuha uses one Red Angus and two Gelbvieh bulls because he is trying to move his herd away from the Simmental breed, which produces large calves that are too big at delivery time.

In the first week of October, Ken weans his new calves and sells his over-wintered steers. At eight months, the steers should weigh about 270 kilograms (600 pounds). Ken usually keeps a few replacement heifers, and back-grounds the rest over the winter. The weaned calves are sent out to summer pasture with the cows.

Begining in January, the cattle start getting their winter feed. Ken shreds large round bales on the home acreage for the cows. The young stock, such as the back-grounded heifers, are fed a grain supplement from bunks in their pens.

Ken and his wife, Jolanne, both teach at the local junior high school. With two solid off-farm incomes, the Yuhas have weathered the BSE crisis far better than ranchers and farmers like Tom Bews, Dave Malinka, and the McKillops whose livelihoods depend on their cattle sales. Ken estimates that he lost from $200 to $300 per head on the cattle he sold in 2004.

These kinds of losses for part-time producers have spin-off effects on the local economy. Ken Yuha, for example, has decided to forgo buying any new farm equipment and replacing his truck. When decisions like these are multiplied by the thousands of part-time farmers in rural

Canada, the effect spreads through their communities. The whole range of businesses that depend on sales to farm families—from equipment and car dealers to insurance companies and appliance retailers—have lost income to the BSE crisis. When farm families are forced to make do with what they have, everyone in their community suffers with them.

CHAPTER 4

Feeding Beef

I t's the business of cow-calf farmers and ranchers to raise calves for finishing by feedlot operators. And their business is all directed toward putting tender, well-marbled, premium-priced beef on the plates of consumers. That involves feeding calves up to market weight on a grain- or corn-based diet that adds muscle and marbling. To make a good profit, feedlot operators must get the fastest rate of gain with the least amount of feed.

Feedlots have changed the beef industry dramatically. Where once it took four years to raise cattle on grassland up to marketable weight, today's feedlots turn out market-ready animals at 18 months of age. This decrease in turn-around time from birth to market means greater profits for ranchers and farmers, who can sell three times the number of animals in four years.

The Value of Marbling

The fine specks and threads of intramuscular fat that appear throughout a cut of lean beef is called marbling. The amount of marbling determines how tender, juicy, and flavourful the beef is, and how it is graded. To receive a top grade—a Prime or Grade A stamp in Canada—the beef must show "abundant marbling." The other major criteria for grading is the animal's age at slaughter. Only calves under the age of 24 months—when their muscles are still tender—are graded as Prime or Grade A. The colour of the fat in beef cuts is important to consumers. They will pay higher prices for white marbling, which is produced by the grain diet that calves are fed in feedlots, than they will for yellow, which comes from the beta-carotene in a grass-based diet. In the agribusiness world, the process of producing beef that meet the criteria that consumers want in order to garner the best profits is called "adding value."

In the days before cattle were finished for market in feedlots, they were finished on grass, usually at the ranch or farm where they were born. The first feedlots date back to the mid-1800s. Their original purpose was to feed animals recovering from long and arduous journeys to prime market areas. One of the best-known cattle drives in the United States followed the Chisholm Trail from Texas to Abilene, Kansas.

After the American Civil War, there was huge demand for beef in the growing cities of the northern and eastern states. Big profits could be made on cattle raised cheaply on Texas prairie grass and then trailed north to the best markets. By the late 1860s, a good price for a four-year-old Texas longhorn was $3 to $4 at home on the range and as much as $40 in Chicago, Philadelphia, and New York.

The cattle were driven slowly, averaging 15 to 30 kilometres (10 to 20 miles) a day. Depending on the size of the herd, the weather, and the skills of the cowboys, a cattle drive of almost 1,300 kilometres (800 miles) could take up to 80 days. The cattle arrived exhausted and thin. Cattle buyers kept them in livestock yards for several months to fatten them on a grain or corn diet until they regained enough weight to ship to meat packers in Chicago.

By the early 1870s, a feedlot industry had sprung up in Kansas and Nebraska to cater to consumers who had developed a preference for tender, well-marbled beef from feedlots, or "fed," cattle over the tougher beef of pasture-raised animals. Feedlots arrived a bit later in Canada. There were a few in Ontario in the latter part of the nineteenth century. They were established by industries that had grain left over from manufacturing such products as beer, flour, and spirits. These breweries, flour producers, and distilleries fed over-wintered cattle on their leftover grain and then sold them to markets in the U.S. and Europe.

Ontario became the hub of the Canadian cattle-feeding business as ranchers in the West shipped their cattle to feedlots in the East for finishing on grain or corn. Some cattle raised in the western provinces were shipped south to U.S. feedlots for finishing. Raising calves in the West and finishing them in the East was standard practice in the Canadian beef industry until the early 1980s—all because of the Crow Rate.

The Crow Rate was a special rate for transporting grain, mainly wheat and barley, to shipping ports for export. Established by the Canadian government in 1897, it was an incentive for the Canadian Pacific Railway to build a second rail line through the mountains to the sea. The new line ran through the Crowsnest Pass between southern Alberta and British Columbia. As part of the federal government's vision of developing western Canada into a major grain-growing area, the rate was set extremely low—initially at a half a cent per ton per mile. That made it feasible for farmers to grow grain on the prairies and ship it to distant ports in Vancouver, Churchill, Manitoba, and the Lakehead in Ontario.

The Crow Rate also made it economically unfeasible for ranchers in the grain-growing belt of the prairie provinces to finish their own calves on grain that was fetching high prices from the world's grain importers. Ranchers could not pay these prices and make a profit on their cattle.

This situation lasted well into the 1970s when the effects of the Crow Rate began to be felt by the railroads.

The very low rates they were receiving for the transportation of grain made the whole enterprise unprofitable. For example, by 1976, the Crow Rate made up only 30 per cent of the actual cost of transporting the grain. The result was that the railroads were not reinvesting in infrastructure to carry the grain and load it onto ships at the ports. As their equipment fell into disrepair, rail lines were less and less able to get the grain where it needed to go, and more and more grain remained on the prairies.

Provincial governments in the West began to realize that finishing cattle close to where the calves were actually raised could become a profitable prairie industry. Several provinces set up programs to subsidize the cost of grain, thus allowing ranchers and farmers to grain-feed their calves up to market weight. Alberta's program was originally called the Feed Grain Market Adjustment Program, and it came into effect in 1985.

In 1983 the federal government passed the Western Grain Transportation Act so that the railroads could begin to recoup the real costs of moving grain. The added cost to the grain farmers made it just as profitable to sell their barley to local ranchers for finishing steers. The Crow Rate itself was finally abolished in August 1995.

Western feedlots began springing up almost overnight. Feedlot owners received additional encouragement from a federal-provincial program called the National Tripartite Stabilization Program. It was essentially an insurance program that paid producers the differential when cattle prices fell below an agreed-upon monthly price. Two-thirds of these paid-out premiums were paid by the federal and provincial governments. The producer took a hit on the final third. Although this program was abandoned in 1993 under pressure from American producers, it had a major influence in getting the feedlot business up and running in western Canada.

◆◆◆◆◆

All feedlots are specialized facilities that confine groups of cattle in pens dominated by feed bunks along one side. A standard pen holds between 100 and 300 animals. Each pen contains calves of the same size, sex, and weight so that they can be fed the same mixture and quantity of a ration. The ration gets changed as the cattle put on weight. The bunks are "read" each morning to determine how much feed is left and how much needs to be added. The key to good profits is to avoid incurring extra costs by over-feeding or over-finishing the calves.

Feedlots need facilities for storing the ingredients that go into their feed and for mixing the ingredients into different rations, depending on a penful of animals' stage of development. Large feedlots in Alberta usually have their own feed mills on the premises with silos full of barley and a silage bunker nearby. Feed trucks or tractors equipped with augurs mix the ration for each pen, manoeuvre down a wide alleyway that runs along one side, and dump the right amount of feed in the bunk.

With such big investments in feed, facilities, and equipment, economies of scale often determine the success of a feedlot. Today, an average feedlot in Ontario finishes between 300 and 1,000 head of cattle. The largest one in the province has the capacity for 5,000 to 7,000 animals. In Alberta, the smaller feedlots have 2,000 to 3,000 cattle, and the larger ones feed between 25,000 and 40,000.

No matter what size, most feedlots follow a similar production process. They all start by filling their pens with calves. Generally, there are three entry points for calves. The first is for "heavies," or calves that are very large at weaning, between 250 and 320 kilograms (600 and 700 pounds). They will be kept in the feedlot for six or seven months. For example, Ken Yuha from Okotoks sends all his calves to the feedlot as heavies; by calving in February, he usually has calves big enough for a feedlot by the first of October. Calves of this size are also called "long-keeps" because they stay in the feedlot for the maximum amount of time. They enter the feedlot in the fall, are fed over the winter, and then are sent for slaughter the following spring when they are around 545 to 590 kilograms (1,200 to 1,300 pounds). At this point, they are usually 12 to 14 months of age. Often the long-keeps have bloodlines from the bigger breeds, such as Charolais or Limousin, but they may be just "big for their age."

The second entry point brings in slightly smaller calves. They weigh between 225 to 270 kilograms (500 and 600 pounds), and are usually animals that have been over-wintered on grass or hay in order to add skeletal size as a background for the later addition of muscle and fat. This backgrounding stage generally lasts three to six months and adds 90 to 135 kilograms (200 to 300 pounds). They will require four or five months of finishing on grain in a feedlot to reach the optimum slaughter weight.

The final point of entry is for calves that are relatively small at weaning, about 160 to 275 kilograms (350 to 500 pounds). These calves are often kept on their home ranch or in a backgrounding operation where they eat grass, hay, or silage, for a full year after weaning. These "long yearlings" are sent to the feedlot in the fall when they are 12 to 18 months of age. They will require only three to four months of feeding to reach slaughter weight, and usually get sold to a packing plant sometime in the winter.

Both steer calves and heifer calves are sold to feedlots. The final weight of heifers is about 7 per cent less than that of steers, and the once common price discount for heifers is now disappearing. Heifers are kept separate from steers and are often given hormones to prevent estrus. Some feedlot operators specialize in either steers or heifers, though the larger feedlots finish both.

Profits for feedlot operators depend on their knowing what, how much, and how long to feed their calves for the best rate of gain. Calves raised on range grasses, supplemented by winter hay, take a lot longer to reach market

Process for Cattle Feeding in Canada

Calving weights (Feb. to April)
British breeds: 35–40kg.
Cross breeds: 40–50kg.
European breeds: 50–60kg.

Weaning weights Oct. to Dec.
180–320 kg.

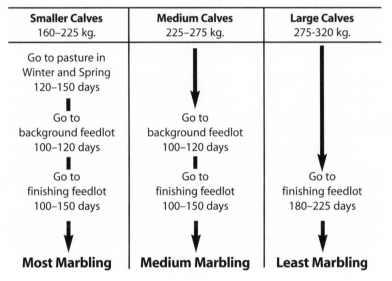

Smaller Calves 160–225 kg.	Medium Calves 225–275 kg.	Large Calves 275-320 kg.
Go to pasture in Winter and Spring 120–150 days		
Go to background feedlot 100–120 days	Go to background feedlot 100–120 days	
Go to finishing feedlot 100–150 days	Go to finishing feedlot 100–150 days	Go to finishing feedlot 180–225 days
Most Marbling	**Medium Marbling**	**Least Marbling**

weight than feedlot calves eating a high-carbohydrate diet based on grain or corn. Feedlots change the diet of calves that have been raised on grass and hay to rations of silage and grain in slow steps because digestive systems need time to adjust. Ruminant stomachs are adapted to break down grasses. When calves are switched too quickly to rations containing the high carbohydrate content of grains or corn, their stomachs may produce too much gas, usually carbon dioxide and methane, and cause a life-threatening condition known as "bloat."

Even under normal circumstances, one beef animal produces an incredible amount of methane, about 550 litres (145 gallons) a day. Usually, gases pass through the cattle gut with the feces or are simply passed through the mouth when the animals belch. An incident in January 2005 on a feedlot near Ponoka, Alberta, underlined how devastating a feeding mistake can be. The feedlot operator had gone bankrupt, and the trustee contracted a private firm to feed the animals until they could be sold. After being fed the wrong mixture of grain and silage, 150 cattle died from bloat.

The amount of grain or corn in a feedlot calf's diet is gradually increased until it forms about 85 per cent of the ration. The ration of long-keeps, or newly weaned calves, is brought up to this level very slowly. At about 400 kilograms (900 pounds), they are still consuming a ration that is half silage and half grain.

The grain or corn is milled to crack the seed coat, which the animals cannot easily digest. A feedlot operator's goal is to have a calf increase its weight by about 1.8 kilograms (4 pounds) a day. Generally, the calves put on about .45 kilograms (1 pound) for every 2.7 kilograms (6 pounds) of feed. Near the end of the feedlot finishing process, a calf is eating about 11 kilograms (24 pounds) of mainly grain or corn each day. A long yearling brought into the feedlot at 400 kilograms (900 pounds) will be up to the standard market weight of 545 to 590 kilograms (1,200 to 1,300 pounds) in about 90 days.

Most feedlots add other ingredients to their cattle rations. Until 1997 when meat and bone meal made from ruminants was banned in Canada, it was often added to cattle feed to increase protein and calcium content, which helped the animals gain weight faster. Protein supplements in feedlot rations are now soy-based.

Animals that are confined in pens in a feedlot have a higher risk of contracting diseases, such as liver abscesses and pneumonia. As a preventative measure, feedlot operators have for many years routinely added antibiotics to their cattle feed, or injected them just under the cattle's skin. This routine use of antibiotics is subtherapeutic, which means it's intended to prevent rather treat diseases. Chlortetracycline, for example, is often used to prevent liver abscesses, bacterial diarrhea, and foot rot—all health issues that could slow down an animal's ability to gain weight efficiently. Even more popular as a feed additive is ionophore, usually an Eli Lilly product called Rumensin. When consumed as part of a high-grain diet, it improves feed conversion, maintains or increases daily gain, and does not affect carcass characteristics. Rumensin is usually used in combination with other antibiotics, such as chlortetracycline or oxytetracycline.

Antibiotics are withdrawn from feedlot rations before the cattle go to slaughter and enter the human food chain. Each antibiotic carries a recommended withdrawal period that reflects how long it takes to clear an animal's system. Despite these precautions, there is considerable concern among scientists that the routine use of these drugs may contribute to the evolution of an antibiotic-resistant strain of bacteria that may be dangerous to humans. Denmark has already banned the subtherapeutic use of these drugs, and other countries, such as Sweden, have restricted their use.

Even more controversial is the use of growth-promoting hormones in feedlots. A tablet containing the hormones is implanted in the skin of the ear when a calf arrives at the feedlot. The tablet contains both natural hormones—estradiol, progesterone, and testosterone—and synthetic hormones—zeranol and trenbolone acetate. Heifers are also given another hormone, melangestrol acetate, in their feed to suppress their reproductive cycle. Among scientists and medical researchers, there is concern that these hormones may cause breast cancer and earlier puberty in girls. Generally, these growth hormones are withdrawn 80 days before an animal goes to slaughter so they have time to clear its system.

Studies to detect these hormones in animal fat have never found them in an animal's system when tested after the 80 days, even with technology capable of detecting one part per billion. Nevertheless, the European Union has prohibited the use of growth hormones in cattle raised by its member countries, and it has banned beef imports from countries like Canada and the U.S. where the use of hormones to enhance the growth of cattle is standard practice in feedlots.

Feedlots have suffered less from the BSE crisis than other segments of the beef production system. This is partly because many feedlot operators have maintained a steady income by selling custom-feeding services to other ranchers and farmers. Also, because the boxed beef sector of the export market closed only for a few months in 2003 and is now fully restored, feedlots have continued to sell their steers and heifers directly to meat packers supplying domestic and export markets. However, the large packers have considerable control over cattle prices, especially since there has been no price competition from U.S. packers. This has resulted in prices of up to $34 per hundredweight less than the American beef producers are being paid for their cattle. Still, the market remains steady as packers continue to purchase live cattle to process into the prime cuts bought up by restaurants and supermarkets.

Where operators have been hurt by the BSE crisis is in the low prices they have received for the feedlot cattle they own. By shifting to more custom work, the feedlots are staying afloat but are not making nearly as much profit as they were before the crisis. These reduced profits come at a difficult time for feedlot operators as they come under increasing pressure from environmental groups and the government to clean up their operations and take measures to protect the environment.

A major problem for feedlots is getting rid of mounds of manure. Traditionally, manure was used as fertilizer and spread on pastures and cropland. While some smaller feedlots still follow this practice, manure disposal is a major problem for most large feedlots. In Alberta, for example, the government requires a feedlot with 10,000 head to spread its manure over 560 hectares (1,400 acres) that are irrigated or 1,130 hectares (2,800 acres) that are not irrigated. That requires a lot of land and expensive equipment, all of which translates into higher costs. Feedlots also face other disposal restrictions. To avoid polluting spring run-off water, it is illegal to spread manure when there is snow on the ground. That means that manure from feedlot pens must be stored until late spring. As environmental issues become more and more important, large feedlots may have to switch to the manure digesting system that's been pioneered by Highland Feeders in Alberta. The technology is still experimental and very costly, and is something provincial governments may have to subsidize if the feedlot manure problem is to be dealt with effectively.

Water is another big problem for feedlots. The daily water requirement for one steer falls between 30 and 35 litres (8 and 9 gallons). For a very large feedlot with 30,000 head of cattle, that adds up to 1.2 million litres (324,000 gallons) of water per day. The same amount would supply a town of 5,000 people with all the water they need for drinking, cooking, washing, flushing, and watering their lawns. Feedlots located in areas where water is scarce can put a stress on supply. This seems to be happening in Lethbridge County in southern Alberta.

Lethbridge County has 35 per cent of the province's feed-lot capacity, or the equivalent of about 325,000 head of feeder cattle. That number of cattle needs almot 10 million litres (2.6 million gallons) of water a day—in an area that's dry and where water supplies are strained.

These problems were around before the first case of BSE was discovered in Alberta, and there is no fast or cheap way of fixing them. But for feedlot operators with fewer profits in their pockets, the BSE crisis has made these problems much harder to solve.

◆◆◆◆◆

Highland Feeders near Vegreville, Alberta, is one of the most advanced feedlots in Canada, and the sixth largest. Its capacity is about 36,000 cattle; in the winter of 2005, it was feeding between 32,000 and 33,000 head. Highland Feeders developed out of a family farm and is now operated by Bern and Mike Kotelko. Their feedlot has 150 pens, each able to hold 300 cattle. The Kotelko brothers finish about 70,000 head of cattle each year. Usually about 50 truckloads of finished cattle per week are shipped to Cargill Foods in High River, Alberta. This arrangement is called a "vertical alliance." Bern and Mike could put their beef up for bids from different buyers; they do not have to sell all their cattle to the same packing plant. But they think their alliance with Cargill Foods allows them to produce a higher quality product because they can gear their operation to satisfying the criteria of just one buyer.

A full cattle pen at the feedlot operated by Highland Feeders near Vegreville, Alberta

At any one time, the Kotelkos will own between 30 per cent and 60 per cent of the cattle in their feedlot. The rest of the animals are being custom fed for other ranchers and farmers, who retain ownership of the cattle in the Highland lot and pay for their feeding and upkeep. Custom feeding is common in feedlots because it provides a steady income to feedlot operators and avoids the risk of dropping cattle prices. While it provides a hedge against low prices, custom feeding means lower profits for feedlot owners when the price of beef rises. Most feedlot operators wisely choose to stock their pens with a mixture of cattle they own, and custom-fed cattle that belong to someone else.

Highland Feeders has about 2,000 hectares (5,000 acres) planted in corn and barley crops, which are fed to the cattle as silage and grain. The Kotelkos find that the sweeter corn silage is better for starting newly weaned calves on feed. The cattle in their feedlot eat 15,000 bushels of grain per day—which is equivalent to the yield of a quarter section of land each day of the year. Bern and Mike have contracts with farmers and grain companies to provide the grain they can't produce on their own land. The feedlot has the capacity to store 100,000 bushels of grain, and 45,000 tonnes of silage.

Bern and Mike Kotelko operate Highland Feeders with the most sophisticated and cutting-edge technology. The feeding of the Highland cattle is a highly computerized operation. Each feed truck is equipped with a laptop computer connected through a wireless network to an office server. Through this network, the feed truck operator determines the exact feed ration required for each pen. The ration ingredients are loaded from the feed mill and silage pit, mixed, and finally delivered to the feed bunks.

Fresh water for the livestock is provided by underground water lines that run from eight wells to all the pens. The feedlot pens were built on a 2.5 per cent slope on clay pack to optimize the drainage of cattle wastes. The wastes flow into a holding pond, which is built on clay to avoid contaminating the water supply.

Highland Feeders from the air. The feed trucks move along the roads in front of the feed bunks, and the cattle move along lanes behind the pens.

In co-operation with the Alberta Research Council and several commercial sponsors, Highland Feeders has just built an environmentally friendly electricity plant that transforms cattle manure into energy, bio-based fertilizers, and reusable water. Called the Integrated Manure Utilization System (IMUS), the process combines anaerobic digestion, biogas utilization, liquid/solid separation, nutrient recovery, and enrichment processes. Methane gas produced through anaerobic digestion is used to generate power and heat. When the electricity plant started operating on May 6, 2005, it was capable of producing 1 megawatt of power, which is enough to supply about 750 households.

Highmark Renewables

The energy-producing wing of Highland Feeders is a company called Highmark Renewables, which is managed by Mike Kotelko. While producing energy for 750 homes, the project's Integrated Manure Utilization System (IMUS) expects to reduce greenhouse gas emissions (GHGs) by 13,500 tonnes per year. Mike has an even bigger vision: "by 2010, 20 IMUS units, each with a 20,000-head capacity, would reduce GHGs by 740,000 tonnes annually.

This process not only generates energy; it also recovers and concentrates nutrients from the digested liquid to produce completely natural fertilizers that are free of pathogens. Water recovered from this process can be used for irrigation. If this electricity-generating project proves to be successful, it will solve one of the most serious problems facing feedlot operations—how to get rid of all the cattle manure safely and economically without harming the environment.

When BSE hit the province and beef prices plummeted, Mike and Bern were able to rely on their hedge of custom feeding other people's cattle. In 2004 they lost money on their own cattle, but were able to survive on income from custom feeding and the sale of silage. In the spring of 2005, Bern and Mike were recommending that owners keep their newly weaned cattle on feed for about 280 days to avoid having to sell them at low market prices. Even that amount of time may not be enough to move beef prices back up to pre-BSE levels, but hope springs eternal in the ranching business.

CHAPTER 5

Meat Packing Plants

B efore their second birthday, calves that are raised on a cow-calf ranch and finished in a feedlot are usually on their way to a meat packing plant. Like feedlot owners, meat packers make their profits by "adding value," in this case by turning live animals into meat. That involves a basic process of slaughtering, butchering, and sometimes processing and packaging.

In early days, all this used to happen right down on the farm, one animal at a time. Today, cattle are slaughtered and butchered in high-speed facilities, some capable of handling more than 4,000 cattle per day. The technology that was used to speed up the slaughter process was originally developed by Canada Packers in the 1940s. Called the Can-Pak system and modified many times over the years, it is still used on all modern kill floors.

The system sends one animal at a time down a narrow chute onto a moving rail, which holds the animal by its chest and sends it along. At the end of the rail, it is quickly and humanely killed by a gun that fires a small bolt deep into its brain. One end of a chain is fastened around the left hind foot, and the other end is attached to a moving chain that gradually lifts the animal up and sends it along. From this point on, the animal never stops moving along on an overhead chain. Workers are stationed at various points and heights along the kill floor, and each has one job to perform as the animals go by at a speed of four per minute. Using mostly automated tools, workers remove the hide, head, and all the internal organs. Then the carcass is split in half, hosed down to remove the blood and bits of fat, and moved into a cooler to chill for about 24 hours. After that it goes to a cutting room to be divided into roasts, steaks, and other cuts.

Despite automation, meat packing jobs are not pleasant. Getting people to perform these dirty, smelly jobs in an environment that is either too hot or too cold can be a huge problem. This is especially true because the majority of these plants are no longer unionized.

Personal Experience

Back in my student days, summer jobs were at a premium and one of the most prized in Kitchener, Ontario, was at Schneider's Meats. I managed to get a job at Schneider's after my second year of university. My enthusiasm waned a bit when I discovered that I was on "the hog kill" on the afternoon shift. That put me in the "gut room" below the kill floor. The intestines, lungs, heart, and all the other internal organs were cut out on the kill floor and dropped through a chute to those of us stationed below. I was the "bung cleaner." That meant I received the large intestine, still warm from the pig's body, and had to place the bung (the anus) over a specially modified water tap and massage the feces out of the intestine. Occasionally, one would have weak spots and would explode, showering me with its smelly contents. The temperature in the room hovered around 32° Centigrade, and the stench was overpowering. Later, I was promoted to "bung puller" — a distinct improvement on my first job. I only had to separate the large intestine from the small one. No rubber gloves, no goggles, or protective gear of any kind. Fortunately, I never got the job of straightening out the small intestine, which occasionally resulted in a handful of intestinal worms. It was horrible work, but at least for me it was all over in three months.

Today there are some medium-sized meat packers in Canada that are owned by Canadians, such as XL Beef in Calgary and Moose Jaw, St. Helen's in Toronto, and Levinoff Meats in Montreal. But for the last decade or so, all the major players in this country's meat packing industry have been American-owned companies. It has taken the closing of the U.S. border following the discovery of the BSE in 2003 to expose how much damage this American domination of the meat packing industry has inflicted on Canadian beef producers.

It all started very differently. In the 1920s, Canadians owned two of the three largest meat packing plants in the country, and competed with a third major player, the Canadian subsidiary of an American giant. Canada Packers was formed in 1927 from a merger between Harris Abattoir, an old and established company that slaughtered 500 animals a week, and William Davies, another major Canadian meat packer. The new company went on to buy the Canadian Packing Company, which made it a major force in the country's beef industry. This was the company that revolutionized kill-floor operations in the 1940s by developing the Can-Pak system, essentially doing for the meat packing business what Henry Ford had done for the auto industry.

Originally based in Toronto, Canada Packers gradually expanded into the West by opening packing plants in St. Boniface, Edmonton, and Vancouver. The company slowly widened its scope and moved into rendering, producing fertilizers, operating tanneries, and manufacturing soap products. Today's meat packing industry shows the same level of vertical integration—owning everything from the raw materials to the plants that produce byproducts.

Pat Burns, one of the most colourful and influential ranchers in Alberta's ranching heyday, started his own meat packing business, P. Burns & Co., in the late 1890s. Originally it was a Calgary-based company that operated only in western Canada. When Canada Packers expanded into the West, Burns answered the challenge by moving into the East. He started buying eastern meat packers, including Dumart's Limited in Kitchener, Ontario, and Modern Packers in Montreal, and ended up a serious, full-fledged competitor of Canada Packers.

Poor management almost broke the company in the 1960s. In 1966 it was taken over by Arthur Child, former vice-president of Canada Packers, with the financial backing of Howard Webster from Montreal. Child was a management genius, who had overseen Canada's meat exports to the U.K. during the Second World War. He quickly turned his new company around. Under Child's leadership, Burns was again in the position of being able to acquire more companies. By the early 1970s, it had meat packing plants scattered across the country, from Montreal to Vancouver.

Arthur Child

From 1992-1995, I had monthly meetings with Arthur Child in his office high up in the PetroCanada Tower in Calgary. On the surface, our meetings were about the Reserve Army unit that Arthur was sponsoring. But our conversations often turned to how Arthur ended up owning one of Canada's largest companies. He had been raised in eastern Ontario in very poor circumstances. Hard work won him a break in the late 1920s when he won a scholarship that sent him off to Queen's University in Kingston, Ontario. He graduated just as the Depression was beginning, and the only job he could find was at Canada Packers.

After teaching himself accounting, Arthur rapidly rose to the position of vice-president of Canada Packers. When the president retired in 1960, he turned over the company to his son. Arthur left to become president of a Saskatoon meat packing company and quickly made it profitable. Six years later, he took over the Burns company as it was faltering. Within a year, it was a profitable business again. Soon afterward, Arthur took the company private and became the sole owner. On my first tour of the Burns boardroom, Arthur laughingly said, "I don't know why I have this—I *am* the board."

The third company that dominated the industry alongside Burns and Canada Packers was Swift Canadian, a subsidiary of the Swift and Company of Chicago. Swift Canadian set up its first meat packing company in 1900 in Toronto. After making huge profits selling meat to Britain during the Second World War, it expanded its operations, first to Calgary and Vancouver and then beyond.

By the 1970s, these three companies had taken firm control of Canada's meat packing industry. Their power over the industry prompted several government inquiries. The Royal Commission on Price Spreads in 1934-35, right in the middle of the Depression, investigated meat packers' control over prices paid ranchers for their cattle. The commission findings implicated the packers, particularly Canada Packers and Swift Canadian, but nothing was ever done. That price-fixing challenge was followed by another from the Restrictive Trade Practices

Commission of 1959-1961. Then in the mid-1980s a Conspiracy to Reduce Competition charge was laid under the Combines Investigation Act. Both investigations concluded that the three meat packing companies, and particularly Canada Packers, were restricting fair trade in the meat industry. While they may have made the companies more careful about making further acquisitions, these challenges and charges had little effect on how the companies conducted business.

Although such attempts by the Canadian government to end unfair practices ended up in failure, they did expose the oligopolistic nature of the industry. Meat packers had power to control prices that cattle and hog producers received, and they used it.

By the 1980s, a lot of Canadian beef was moving to the U.S. for processing because the three Canadian companies had abandoned the slaughtering end of the meat packing business, declaring the process unprofitable and leaving the field to much smaller companies. During the 1970s operations diversified into conglomerates, with products ranging from packaged meat to soap and leather, all three found that their profits from the kill floors were marginal at best, largely because of increasing labour costs after plant unionization in the late 1920s and early 1930s. As workers' wages went up, the packers' profits went down.

There were several costly labour strikes as plant workers demanded higher wages that could not be met. In 1978, for example, a seven-week strike at Canada Packers cost the firm several million dollars. A strike at Burns Foods in Calgary in 1984 resulted in the permanent closing of the plant. Arthur Child had warned the workers that the plant was old and unprofitable and that he would have to close it if they went on strike for higher wages. They did, and he did.

Another factor in the decision of the three companies to abandon the slaughtering business was the high cost of maintaining plant equipment. Rapid advances in technology continually made current equipment obsolete. Profits were not sufficient to justify frequent capital expenditures. The companies could not increase production speed, and thus volume to keep up with labour costs.

Per capita Beef consumption in Canada 1960–1999

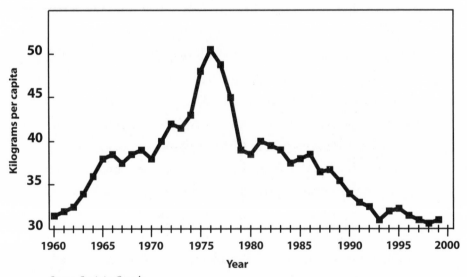

Source: Statistics Canada

Meat packers also faced a drop in consumer demand for beef. Retail beef consumption dropped rapidly after a peak of 38 kilograms (84 pounds) per person in 1975, although for a few years between 1978 and 1983 it stablized to about 30 kilograms (64 pounds), before continuing to drop to the current level of about 22 kilograms (48 pounds). As the demand for beef dropped, cattle herds were cut back, increasing competition among packing plants for slaughter animals. The result was higher cattle prices, and still lower profits for meat packers.

All these changes in the industry forced Canada Packers, Burns and Co., and Swift Canadian to start closing their plants in the 1980s and early 1990s. Other meat

Canadian Beef cow numbers: 1970 to 2008 (projected)

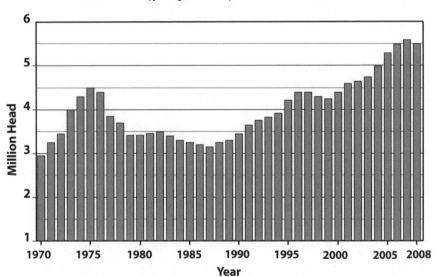

packers followed their lead. Since 1985 and 2005, as many as 21 meat packing plants have closed in Canada. After years of trying to get out of the unprofitable slaughtering business, Canada Packers bought Maple Leaf Mills in 1990 to acquire its processed meat brands. The Canada Packers name was then changed to Maple Leaf Foods which, in 1995, was bought by Wallace McCain and the Ontario Teachers Pension Plan. Maple Leaf then picked up Burns Foods in 1996 after Burns had acquired Gainers in 1993.

Large American corporations, with cheaper labour and much higher volumes, filled the void.

The first American meat packer to move into Canada was Cargill Foods of Minnesota. Using a model developed in the U.S., based on high-speed technology, low labour costs, locations in close proximity to suppliers, Cargill's meat packing division, Excel, established a new operation just outside High River, Alberta, in 1989.

Cargill Foods is a massive food conglomerate with yearly sales of $48 billion. A vertically integrated company, it owns grain storage and sales facilities, fertilizer plants, trucking companies, sweetener companies, and specialty meats brands, as well as steel, petroleum, and natural plants. Cargill is still privately owned by members of the original Cargill family whose first business was a grain storage company founded in 1865, in Minnesota.

Cargill chose High River because the city has ready and close access both to the huge cattle supplies in southern and central Alberta, and to the large labour force in near-by Calgary. Most of Cargill's unionized workers are immigrants. The High River plant was originally designed to process 6,000 head of cattle a week at a speed of about 160 cattle per hour. Within 10 years, this had increased to 260 head per hour, or 3,850 per day. By the fall of 2005, Excel's daily capacity was up to 5,000 head.

In 1989, at the time the High River plant was built, ranchers were sending over 20,000 cattle a week to American slaughter facilities. The exodus of fed cattle to American meat packers began to slow down when the High River plant opened, but Cargill still did not accept cull cattle, which continued to be slaughtered either in smaller local plants or in the U.S. Recently, Cargill purchased Better Beef in Guelph, Ontario, the province's largest slaughter house with a capacity to handle 1,800 head of cattle a day.

While Cargill was the first large U.S. company to enter the Canadian meat packing scene, it was not alone for long. In 1994, IBP Corporation, originally Iowa Beef Producers based in Denison, Iowa, purchased a large beef agribusiness called Lakeside Farm Industries, in Brooks, Alberta. This company owned both a large feedlot and a meat packing business called Lakeside Packers. While IBP was originally a much smaller company than Cargill, by 1999 it had become the largest red-meat processor in the world with sales of over $14 billion. IBP specializes in the latest kill-floor technology, and pioneered the boxed beef concept, which involves cutting beef carcasses into prime cuts, packing the cuts in plastic wrap, and shipping boxes of individual beef cuts to its customers. Like Cargill, IBP used a lower wage structure to keep costs down. Based in a town of just 12,000 people, labour is a huge problem for Lakeside Packers. The company actively recruits immigrants, mostly from the Sudan and Somalia. The employees belong to a union, which remains relatively weak, and Lakeside's job turnover is very high as workers move out of the low-paying, messy positions on the kill floor to find better prospects in Calgary or Edmonton.

When IBP purchased Lakeside Packers, the plant was already very large, with a slaughter capacity of 11,000 head per week. Within three years, Lakeside was moving animals through the kill floor at a rate of 370 head per hour, considerably faster than the Cargill plant. By 1999 the plant was killing 27,600 head per week, which amounts to about 1.4 million head per year.

In 2001, IBP was taken over by Tyson Foods of Springdale, Arkansas, at the time, the world's largest producer of chicken and chicken products. Thus Tyson-IBP-Lakeside became the largest beef, pork, and chicken producer in the world. Sales in 2003 amounted to more than $23 billion. The company is now in the process of completing a $17 million expansion, which will boost daily slaughter capacity to 5,000 fed steers and heifers a day. Like Cargill, Tyson-IBP-Lakeside does not accept cull cattle for slaughter.

Cargill and Tyson now handle over 90 per cent of the Canadian cattle supply. They also have a considerable market share of the beef sold to supermarkets. Lakeside Packers is the exclusive supplier of meat to Safeway, where Cargill supplies National Grocers, the chain that includes Loblaws, Great Canadian Superstore, and Extra Foods.

There are growing concerns in the ranching industry about Cargill's and Tyson's purchasing power and about their ability to control market prices. To date, the government has made no move to investigate either company's business practices, a situation that seems to be a direct result of the BSE crisis, which created an urgent need for slaughter capacity in Canada. Both Cargill and Tyson are increasing their slaughter facilities and taking some pressure off Canadian ranchers. All beef producers, however must still contend with the thorniest problem created after BSE closed the U.S. border—finding slaughter facilities for cull cattle.

CHAPTER 6

BSE and
the Beef Bans

Canadian beef producers lost about $5 billion in the 18 months following the discovery of the first case of domestic BSE on May 20, 2003, according to economists with the BMO Financial Group. On its own, the closing of the U.S. border to live Canadian cattle and all beef products created about $2 billion in losses. But the scope of the BSE crisis goes far beyond one border closing and billion-dollar losses to producers.

Export bans of Canadian beef have taken a serious toll on all segments of the beef industry, from independent ranchers and corporate feedlots to meat packers and renderers, and on all the businesses that depend on them, from livestock truckers to feed companies. The impact has been felt right through the Canadian agricultural industry, especially among dairy farmers, and sheep and hog producers. Perhaps the most difficult consequences to estimate are the economic losses to the rural communities where ranchers and farmers do business. When farmers and ranchers are forced to tighten their belts in order to avoid economic ruin, their decision is felt all the way down the line, from equipment dealers and appliance stores to hairdressers and bowling alleys. All these repercussions from one diseased cow add up to a significant effect on the Canadian economy.

Most of the effects have been the result of the closing of the American border to Canadian cattle and beef products, but the U.S. was only one among a host of countries that took some kind of trade action against Canadian beef. By June 3, 2003, the following 41 countries had placed bans on cattle and cattle-related products from Canada:

Antigua	Guatemala	Russia
Argentina	Hong Kong	Saudi Arabia
Australia	Indonesia	Serbia
Bahamas	Jamaica	Singapore
Barbados	Japan	Slovenia
Brazil	Korea	South Africa
Chile	Latvia	Taiwan
China	Lithuania	Trinidad & Tobago
Colombia	Malaysia	Turkey
Costa Rica	Mexico	Ukraine
Croatia	New Zealand	United States
Cuba	Panama	Uruguay
El Salvador	Peru	Vietnam
European Union	Philippines	

Most of these countries were not major export markets, but the cumulative losses to beef producers amounted to about $28 million a week.

The number of beef products affected by trade actions is long and diverse, and it accounts for a dramatic economic impact on many different segments of the Canadian economy. Here for example, is a partial list of products banned by the United States at the beginning of the BSE crisis:

- live ruminants (imports and transits)
- ruminant meat and meat products
- processed animal protein, such as meat and bone meal, meat meal, bone meal, blood meal, protein meal
- animal feed
- pet food
- milk replacers containing animal fat or non-milk animal protein
- ruminant blood and blood products
- animal vaccines containing ruminant-derived products
- ruminant offal
- ruminant casings
- ruminant glands
- ruminant gland extracts or derivatives
- unprocessed ruminant fat
- processed fats and oils

- nutritional supplements containing specified risk materials (SRMs)
- ruminant bones
- tankage (animal residues that remain after rendering fat in a slaughterhouse, used for fertilizer or feed)
- tallow
- ruminant-derived gelatin for animal use
- ruminant-derived cartilage
- non-hide derived collagen
- ruminant-urine derivatives

The full force of these bans was felt from May 20, 2003, until September 11, 2003, when the U.S. lifted its import restrictions on boxed beef. Mexico also began re-importing boxed beef and pledged to follow the U.S. decisions for lifting further bans. Export markets also reopened for some beef products in a number of other countries, such as Hong Kong, Cuba, New Zealand, Russia, and Macao.

Japan, one of Canada's biggest export markets in Asia, still remains completely closed to all Canadian (and American) beef products. This situation, which is unlikely to change anytime soon, is the direct result of Japan's own BSE crisis. The first case of the disease showed up in the Japanese cattle herd in September 2001, and, since then, about 20 animals have tested positive for BSE. Japan responded to consumer fears of contracting vCJD by instituting rigorous BSE-testing policies, involving the testing of all slaughtered cattle. Now, Japan allows beef imports only from countries that follow its own every-animal testing program, or which can guarantee that beef products come from animals under 21 months of age. So far, neither Canada nor the U.S. has agreed to these stipulations. Both countries argue that they have appropriate surveillance and testing programs in place to ensure the safety of their beef, and that the science of their current BSE risk assessments does not justify the costs of testing all cattle. Canada is moving rapidly to establish a cattle identification program that will allow tracking of all animals from birth to slaughter, which means that the age of an animal can be guaranteed. But whether this new initiative will be enough to convince Japan to accept Canadian beef imports remains to be seen.

The full impact of the loss of these non-U.S. markets is hidden in the mark-up, or value-added, figures of Canadian beef products exported prior to May 2003. Some countries paid through-the-roof prices for specific products. For example, short ribs selling for $2 to $3 per pound in Canada could bring as much as $10 to $12 a pound in Korea, where the entire North American short rib production was sold before the crisis. Today, short ribs are being sent to the "trim" section at meat packing plants where they are ground into hamburger, a relatively low-profit item.

Beef products and parts that Canadians either take for granted or won't eat are highly prized by consumers in other countries. Before BSE, beef products that could not be sold at home, or that brought only a small mark-up, were sold for a large premium in export markets. Such items included beef tongue, kidney, tripe (stomach), feet, and tails. Now these products cannot be sold anywhere. Instead of making large profits from these products in the Asian market, meat packers are now paying to ship them to rendering plants.

According to the Canadian Beef Export Federation, the value difference between having markets for Canadian offal (the waste parts of a butchered animal) and thin meats (flat muscles from the flank and plate brisket) is about $192 per animal. When Canadian beef export markets in Asia were open, meat packers made considerably more profit on each animal destined for that market, even though exports to Asia were far below the numbers going across the border to the United States. About 84 per cent of Canadian beef exports ended up in the American market, which left a seemingly insignificant 16 per cent going to other countries. However, the figures for the amounts of beef exported to other countries, especially Japan, do not indicate how valuable these markets were, nor how much the Canadian beef industry has lost since these markets imposed export bans.

The brunt of the economic damage from the widespread bans on Canadian exports has obviously fallen hardest on the ranching sector. (The figures for 2002 are lower than they were two years earlier because hay and

Canada's Beef and Cattle Exports, 2004

Canada exported 455 million kilograms (about 1 billion pounds) in 2004. About 84 per cent went to the U.S.; about 19 per cent to Mexico; and about 3 per cent to Asia.

forage production suffered during two consecutive dry summers.) The report indicates that, in 2002, farm cash receipts from cattle and calves totalled nearly $8 billion, or made up 21 per cent of the Canadian total of $36 billion in farm cash receipts.

In 2000, beef cattle farms accounted for $11 billion, or 29 per cent, of total Canadian agricultural production. Statistics Canada commissioned a report in June 2004, entitled "Canada's Beef Cattle Sector and the Impact of BSE on Farm Family Income." From these figures alone, it's clear that beef exports made up a significant portion of overall farm operations and filled an important part of the Canadian economy.

The post-BSE picture is dramatically different. In 2003, income from cattle and calves dropped to an estimated $5.2 billion, a 33 per cent change from the previous year, and in 2004 the income rose to only $6.3 billion.

The Statistics Canada report focused mainly on the plight of ranchers and their families. In the year 2000, it estimated that there were 71,050 farms with revenues of $10,000 or more that were classified as beef cattle farms.

Of these farms, 49,680 derived at least half of their income from cattle. Across Canada the average total income for this group was just under $60,000.

On the basis of operating income, Statistics Canada divided beef operations into small, medium, large, and very large farms. By the end of 2003, it estimated that there had been a 35 per cent decline in cattle and calf revenues, and a 20 per cent decline in beef cattle replacement costs. As the income of ranchers declined, so did the cost of on-farm inventory. It was on this basis that the total income lost for each category of ranch was calculated.

The hardest hit ranches were those operating very large, intensive cattle operations (ranches like the Big Loop

Beef Facts: 2004

- 65 per cent of Canada's beef farms had fewer than 7 cows

- 25 per cent of Canada's beef farms had between 47 and 122 beef cows

- 10 per cent of Canada's beef farms had more than 122 beef cows, or 40 per cent of the beef cow herd

- Canadian producers finished about 3.4 million calves to market weight

- The Canadian cattle industry produced about 1.5 billion kilograms (3.2 billion pounds) of beef

Source: Canfax; Statistics Canada

Cattle Company that Tom Bews runs in the foothills of Alberta) wherein the average annual loss for each, for the year 2003, was estimated to be $220,000. A large operation, like the one Dave Malinka owns near Vegreville, Alberta, was estimated to have lost around $36,000, while losses for the kind of small to medium-sized operations run by Ken Yuha near Okotoks, Alberta, were estimated to be between $6,000 and $15,000. Although these figures are merely averages based on size of each operation, their implications are clear: the larger the ranch, the greater the loss. Even more revealing is that, based on 4 per cent of farm families reporting a negative income in 2000, some 10 per cent of these ranchers had a negative family income in 2003. This figure includes off-farm income from couples working full or part-time in other jobs. Added to this are another 50 per cent who had a positive family income, but who lost money from their farming operations in 2003. In 2003 the number of ranchers earning over $60,000 in total income dropped from 39 per cent to 26 per cent.

While the situation improved somewhat in 2004, income from ranching still had not reached pre-BSE levels. Instead of the 35 per cent drop in cattle revenue that farm families suffered between 2002 and 2003, the drop from 2002 was 21 per cent in 2004. Based on the averages from 2003, this means that the very large operations (about 4.3 per cent of the total number of ranches deriving at least half of their family income from beef) lost a further $133,570 in income during 2004. Large farms, about 28 per cent of the total, lost another $21,860, and medium-sized farms, about 23 per cent of the ranches, another $9,100 loss. Small farms, some 44 per cent of total operations, suffered more additional losses of $3,650. To get a better perspective on what these figures have meant for farm families, imagine that your boss tells you that you will have to take a 35 per cent cut in salary this year and another 21.25 per cent from the same base salary the next year. This is what the beef farmers experienced over 2003 and 2004, when cattle prices plummeted.

Early 2005 brought a brief price spurt, as markets anticipated reopening of the U.S. border on March 7; these prices quickly evaporated when the border remained closed. Meat packer prices for fed cattle, what the industry calls "fats," in 2002 ranged from $109.20 per hundredweight (an industry term for 100 pounds, usually abbreviated to cwt), or just over $1.09 a pound, to $115.13 per hundredweight. In the early part of 2005, prices edged close to this level, but fell back to about $78.25 a hundredweight on June 6, a 28 per cent price drop from 2002. Ranchers who chose to have their cattle custom fed by feedlot operators were hit especially hard. Ranchers fortunate enough to have sold their calves in January or February 2005, were not as badly hurt, but ranchers having to sell in the months until the border reopened, lost larger amounts of money.

We have mentioned several times the serious problems created by the lack of a cattle cull market for Canadian cows. Ranchers have long depended on money from the sale of cull cattle to top up what they earn from selling beef calves. Cattle cull money was often spent on repairing old buildings and replacing old equipment.

Traditionally, cull cattle have been worth between $700 and $800 per specimen, depending upon grade. Prime beef from fed cattle is graded from AAA down, depending on the muscling and marbling of the animal. The highest grade for mature cattle is D1, and from there grading goes down with the quality of the culled cow or bull from D2 to D4. In the spring of 2005, D1 and D2 cows were being traded at $15 to $27 per hundredweight or, for the average-sized cull cow of about 590 kilograms (1,300 pounds), between $195 and $350. The market is about the same for cull bulls, with prices ranging between $18 and $29 per hundredweight.

Prices for cull cattle have become largely irrelevant for ranchers. Since the BSE crisis, most of them have been unable to find a buyer for these animals. Nor can cull cattle be shipped to buyers in the U.S., where a huge number of them used to be sent for slaughter. Few meat packing plants in Canada have the time or capacity to slaughter and butcher these animals. And even if Canadian meat packers did have time and capacity, they are not about to cut profits by processing less valuable meat with no visible market. The average annual

Canadian cull rate is 11 per cent, per beef herd. Thus the number of culled cattle here per year is around 450,000.

Since there are few buyers for these cull animals, herd owners have little choice but to keep them on the farm, hoping for one more calf from the cows or at least some action from the bulls. Whether successful or not, these animals have to be fed, so rather than adding money to farm family coffers as they did in the past, culls end up increasing farm costs. According to Statistics Canada, the Canadian cattle herd stood at 15.1 million head as of January 1, 2005, an increase of 1.6 million head from two years earlier. This increase is certainly not because ranchers are keeping more feeder cattle.

Many farms and small ranches are being sold and farm families are being uprooted, often from land that has been part of their families for generations. The cattle business has always had ups and downs, but the last five years—two years of drought followed by BSE—have discouraged many sons and daughters from taking over the family farm operation. Wealthy oilmen and large conglomerates are buying land from families who have become discouraged or gone bankrupt. This will certainly change the future landscape of rural ranching country. Government support programs and bank loans have kept larger ranchers afloat, so far, but the severity of this crisis caused even these people to reconsider their future in the cattle business.

Feedlot operators who buy calves from ranchers are another group that's been doing some reconsidering since

BSE hit the industry and closed export markets. Feedlots pay more per pound for the feeder cattle than they receive for the finished product, but count on the lower cost of weight gain to make their profits. For example, as of June 2005, feedlot operators were buying calves weighing about 270 kilograms (600 pounds), designated "heavies" in the trade, for between $107 and $117 a hundred-weight, and selling them for $78.25 a hundredweight. The profit for the feedlot in this case comes from adding 320 kilograms (700 pounds) to an animal bought for $660, and selling it for $1,017. Costs of feeding the animal for seven months, as well as other such operating expenses as labour and fuel must be deducted from the selling price. Prices for finished calves ready for market have dropped considerably since the start of the BSE crisis, so feedlots feeding their own cattle are making significantly less.

Most feedlot operators are also in the business of custom feeding cattle that belong to other people, including independent ranchers, private investors, and meat packers. Custom feeding has been an important way for feedlot operators to maintain a relatively decent income when they have lost money on sales of their own cattle because of low prices. That too has been affected by the trade bans that came with the BSE crisis. The number of cattle in feedlots immediately after May 20, 2003, dropped dramatically. According to Canfax, the Canadian Cattlemen's Association market analysis division, in 2002 there were

1,077,343 cattle on feed in Alberta and Saskatchewan. In 2004, after the closing of the border, there were only 791,466 on feed in these provinces. According to the Canadian Animal Health Coalition, this resulted in a loss of $192 million dollars to the feedlot industry within just a few months of the discovery of Alberta's first BSE case.

Since 2004, the number of cattle on feed has recovered considerably. As of April 1, 2005, there were 974,403 cattle on feed, but all figures indicate that most feedlots are now operating well under their capacity.

Feedlots do have the ability to hold off putting their cattle to market until prices improve by placing them on maintenance rations, which slow down the rate of body mass gain. However, this strategy is limited. Once cattle pass 590 kilograms (1,300 pounds), or whatever the ideal "hook weight" of the meat packing plant is (and rarely over 635 kilograms or 1,400 pounds)—then the price for finished cattle drops, and sometimes the plant will not even accept the animal for processing. Feedlot operators are left with only a small window of time, and if the U.S. border does not open before that window closes, they are stuck selling their animals at a loss.

Few ranchers or feedlot operators have any sympathy for meat packers, because theirs is the only segment of the beef industry still making money—lots of it in fact. Both Cargill and Tyson Foods are currently running at full capacity, six days a week, two shifts a day, in order to keep up with the demand for "hook space." Both are expanding their capacity as rapidly as possible to keep up with supply. Tyson is spending $17 million to upgrade its Lakeside plant in Brooks, and Cargill has instituted a similarly aggressive expansion. Slaughtering services are in such great demand that neither firm takes in lower-profit cull cattle. Their meat packing facilities are entirely focused on slaughtering fed cattle, not only because these are the bigger moneymakers, but also because the U.S. Department of Agriculture arbitrarily ruled older cattle cannot be slaughtered in the same facility as younger cattle. This stipulation must be adhered to stringently if meat packers want to export boxed beef to the U.S.

Before the border closed, 30 to 40 per cent of cull cattle or between 210,000 and 280,000 cows and bulls each year were slaughtered in the U.S. Canada lacked the plant facilities to take these animals. This same lack of capacity also made it necessary for fed cattle to be sent south to slaughter, some being trucked as far as Kansas or Nebraska. In 2002 a total of 14,535 head of fed cattle flooded over the border each week. The border closing has meant that more than one million head of Canadian cattle killed in the U.S. per year have to be killed somewhere else, as the Canadian domestic market still needs beef. The boxed beef industry is actually shipping more to the U.S. than it did before the BSE crisis. Hence, the huge demand for Canadian hook space and the happy state of affairs for meat packers in Canada.

As rosy as their situation is, meat packers also have had some losses and increased costs dumped into their laps by both BSE and export bans. Initially, the meat packers lost money when the border was closed entirely, from May 20 to September 11, 2003, to both live animals and boxed beef. Because packers had already purchased fed cattle, usually through forward contracts with feedlots, and then had no place to sell the beef once the demands of the domestic market were satisfied, they took a total loss by donating over 1.5 million pounds of beef to food banks across Canada.

Another loss resulted when beef products already sent to export markets but not yet distributed were refused; $12 million worth of beef in Korea and Japan was not able to be distributed once the first BSE cow had been discovered. This inventory, plus subsequent warehousing and disposal costs, added up to a total of over $50 million in direct losses to meat packers.

Before Canada's first case of BSE showed up, renderers paid meat packers for offal, or the unusable parts of the animal. Today the situation has reversed, as meat packers now pay renderers to remove the offal from their facilities. This new state of affairs is the result of the Canadian government's decision to ensure that BSE-infected meat does not end up on consumers' plates. In 2004, the government prohibited the use of Specified Risk Materials (SRM)—the parts of cattle that carry the BSE agent—in all meats produced for human consumption. Animal parts included are the skull, brain, trigeminal ganglia (nerves attached to the brain), eyes, tonsils, spinal cord, and dorsal root ganglia of cattle aged 30 months or more, as well as the distal ileum (part of the small intestine) of cattle of all ages. All this material must be removed from the carcass during processing, and rendering companies can no longer use any of this material for any edible products produced for human or animal consumption. SRM can only be used in lower-profit inedible products, such as candle and soap products, and because renderers are not willing to pay for this material, meat packers must now compensate them to haul it away. Hauling blood to a rendering facility, for example, costs meat packers about $200 per truckload.

It is not just the nature of the material that is causing a problem; it is the sheer volume. Meat packers are processing so many animals that rendering companies are overwhelmed. In addition, there are very few rendering plants in the country. Alberta, for example, has just three, Ontario has five. When the supply of any product overwhelms demand, the price plummets. Today, the price is negative, and the packers pay for enormous volumes of offal to be removed and recycled.

There is also a considerable volume of offal that even renderers don't want. Meat packers must either burn or dump this material in landfills, again at added cost. All aspects of this waste problem have added to the cost of killing beef and breaking the carcasses. These costs are built into the price that the packers are willing to pay for cattle, or are tacked on to the price of the meat.

Meat packers have redesigned their slaughter process so that SRM can be safely removed and disposed of. In carcasses of animals over 30 months of age, for example, the entire spinal cord is cut out and disposed of, a process which requires more workers and changes in rail procedures. These added meat packing costs are often passed on to wholesalers and supermarkets, who in turn pass them on to their customers, all a direct result of Canada's first case of BSE.

Despite the increases in capacity that should be online by the fall of 2005, it is questionable whether either Tyson or Cargill will process cull cattle in the future. Smaller meat packers, like XL Beef's Calgary plant still slaughter cull beef, but their Moose Jaw plant (which is also increasing its capacity) has switched over to processing fed cattle only. A solution to the problem of what to do with the cull cattle glut may possibly be found in some of the newer processing plants just starting up. Blue Mountain Packers in Salmon Arm, B.C., for example, has reopened under new ownership and is processing cull cows and bulls, but so far has slaughter capacity for only 50 head a day.

While most of the meat packers' losses and increased costs are being passed back to the producer or forward to the consumer, some write-offs were taken. Overall, however, the packers have been sitting in the most fortunate position during the whole BSE crisis, reaping big profits as a result of the export bans on Canadian beef.

This is not the case for the rendering business. Rendering facilities have been flooded with material from the meat packers, in addition to accepting bone and fat from supermarkets, dead animals from farms, roadkill, and pets. Because renderers are now charging meat packers for the removal of SRM and other slaughter wastes, they have a new source of income.

In 1997 the Canadian and American governments placed a ban on feeding ruminant-derived products back to ruminants. That meant that meat and bone meal, one of the rendering industries' main products, could not be made from cattle or sheep, or from ruminant roadkill (deer, elk, or moose). Such material could only be used in poultry or pig feed. Renderers ceased accepting dead deer and elk, as well as sheep over 12 months of age.

When the first Canadian cow tested positive for BSE in 2003, problems in the Canadian rendering industry began to escalate. The loss of all export markets for meat and bone meal (MBM), especially in the United States, eliminated a huge source of revenue for the rendering industry. On hand stocks of MBM were immediately worthless and had to be dumped in landfills (along with roadkill animals). China, Korea, and Europe closed their borders to exports of meat meal, poultry meal, feather meal, and tallow (another major rendering product). Taiwan also stopped importing Canadian tallow.

The future of Canada's rendering industry remains highly uncertain. There has been considerable talk of a comprehensive ban of all animal protein from all feed products. Such a step would virtually eliminate an important income source, because much of the cheap dead meat ending up in rendering plants is used in protein supplements for pig and chicken feed. Should such a ban of animal protein ever become reality, renderers will end up adding this material to the offal and the SRM they now truck to incinerators and landfills.

When ruminant parts were banned from cattle feed, in 1997, feed companies were forced to change their production lines so that meat and bone meal meant for cattle was kept separate from similar feed destined for pigs and poultry. Feed manufacturers had to ensure that no ruminant material ended up in cattle feed. The scope of this challenge was highlighted by the inspection of the feed companies that the Canadian Food Inspection Agency conducted in 2004. Test results were reported in January 2005. Tests of 110 samples of feed, both imported and domestic, found animal material in 66 of them. Some of this material apparently came from ruminants. The amounts were microscopic, so the problem did not seem to be a result of deliberate non-compliance with the government's regulations. More likely, this was an issue of cross-contamination, bits of ingredients destined for poultry and pig feed accidentally ending up in cattle feed.

In order to keep all the raw components of the various feeds completely separate, feed companies have two choices, both involving costly changes. Either they can thoroughly clean production lines between production runs of different animal feeds, or they can maintain entirely separate lines for each species. There is much pressure on these companies from organizations, such as the Canadian Health Coalition, to follow the European model and place a complete ban on using animal protein in animal feed. This is a costly proposition, one that requires switching from animal protein to protein from much more expensive vegetable sources, such as soy.

Although it may be hard for beef producers to muster much sympathy for feed companies, rendering plants, and the meat packing industry, they can easily commiserate with hog producers, dairy farmers, sheep farmers, truckers, veterinarians, and local equipment dealers. These people are often their neighbours, friends, and business associates sharing rural communities.

Before BSE, trucking cattle was a highly lucrative business. In fact, the truckers often made more money than the ranchers did from the cattle business. Transporting cattle by rail ceased about 20 years ago. Nowadays all are moved from one area to another in open-sided cattle liners. The mainstay of the industry is trucking cattle to and from auctions and feedlots, and from feedlots to meat packing plants. This aspect of the industry has not been affected. However, truckers hauling live animals over the U.S. border, often to plants as far away as Greeley, Colorado, have been devastated by the border closing, as some 22,000 annual hauls (what it took to transport the one million cattle exported to the U.S. each year) have been lost.

In a survey taken by the Canadian Cattlemen's Association in early 2005, the trucking industry in Canada indicated that it had suffered a drop of between 25 and 40 per cent in available loaded miles since May 20, 2003, a loss which has resulted in the attrition of power units and trailers through sale or repossession. Many experienced drivers have even walked away from the cattle industry. Alberta drivers have been able to find jobs in the red-hot oil industry, but that has not been the case throughout Canada. Some people in the industry predict that there will not be sufficient transportation for cattle when the U.S. border does eventually reopen to live animals.

BSE may be a beef problem, but the fallout has resulted in huge losses for dairy farmers. Again, the biggest problem has been what to do with cull cows. Like their cousins in the beef herds, dairy cattle wear out. A dairy cow is productive for an average of five years. This makes the cull rate of dairy cows as high as 25 per cent, more than twice the 11 per cent rate on the beef side. Since there is very little slaughter capacity for these animals, and no export market available for the hamburger and sausages produced from their meat, even if kill space was available, dairy farmers are stuck with unproductive culls. According to TD Financial, this problem translates into a 20 per cent loss of income per annum for the sector. (Other sources give estimates in the 10 per cent range.) Like their beef counterparts, in many cases, it is the sale of cull animals that provides a dairy farmers' net annual profit.

Before BSE, another source of income for dairy farmers was the sale of veal calves. Only about 3.5 per cent of male calves born to dairy cows end up as bulls; the rest become either veal calves or steers for the beef industry. Male calves that are destined for the veal market are removed from their mothers just a few days after birth. They are fed milk substitutes until they are slaughtered at 18 to 20 weeks of age. Generally, veal prices are high because of the meat's tenderness and premium taste. Before the beef ban, veal calves were trucked to the U.S. and slaughtered in meat packing facilities especially designed for 500-pound calves. Now it's almost as difficult to get veal calves slaughtered in Canada as it is to get cull cattle killed. There is simply not enough kill capacity for the smaller veal animals because lines in most meat packing plants are usually designed for finished calves of some 1,300 pounds. Any veal animals that do make it to slaughter in Canada, end up in the smaller packing facilities, a factor which increases prices to consumers.

An equally serious problem has been the loss of sales of dairy breeding stock to the U.S. Embryo sales, as well, have been curtailed to some countries. Both losses have further depressed the dairy industry's profit picture. Milk consumers have been directly affected. The price of milk has been increased twice since the early days of the BSE crisis, despite grants available from the cull cattle program.

BSE has affected hog producers as well. The demand for Canadian pork has dropped, not because of any danger that pork consumption poses to human health, but because many consumers, especially in overseas markets, stopped eating meat from hogs raised on feed containing animal protein, some of it from cattle, sheep, and other ruminants. Although there is no known risk to consumers eating pork products from animals that have been fed ruminant-based meat and bone meal, many consumers have refused to buy pork.

Some pork processors have responded to these consumers by changing their rules. Maple Leaf Pork in Brandon, Manitoba, for example, will not take hogs that have been fed meat and bone meal, neither does Ontario Pork. As more processors follow their lead, the Canadian Pork Council has calculated that costs for hog farmers will increase at least $4.71 per hog if rendered proteins are banned, and a massive $25.33 per hog if all animal byproducts are removed from both the human and the pet food chains. These increased costs will come from having to raise hogs on more expensive non-rendered feed and from losing markets (in the rendering industry and the pet food industry) for hog offal left over from the slaughtering process. This loss plus increased costs of non-rendered hog feed, will lead to higher prices for pork products.

Like beef producers, hog produces are also stuck with the costs of disposing of those dead animals that used to be welcome in rendering plants. Most renderers have stopped accepting animals dead from disease or old age.

When the U.S. border closed to cattle, it also closed to other ruminants, such as sheep, goats, and bison, despite the fact that there was no scientific evidence that these animals posed any threat to human health. The effect on Canadian sheep producers was immediate. The closed border ended the export of about 100,000 heavy lambs a year. (American consumers prefer heavier lambs, weighing around 140 pounds; Canadian consumers like their lambs smaller, at about 100 pounds.) In the first half of 2004 alone, sheep producers saw a drop of about 35 per cent in revenue. There are no support programs specifically designed for lamb producers, as there are for beef producers, although some help is available from the Canadian Agricultural Income Stabilization Program.

Large-animal veterinarians who are in the business of treating cattle, hogs, and sheep have been affected by the BSE crisis, but in a more indirect manner. Ranchers are not calling their local vets as often as they did prior to BSE. Many ranchers have resorted to treating health problems in their herds as best they can. Some watch and wait, hoping the problem heals itself. Others just bury an animal when it dies.

On March 15, 2004, almost one year into the BSE crisis, Dr. Randy Graham, the vice-president of the

Ontario Association of Bovine Practitioners, told a reporter with the *Guelph Mercury* that the large-animal veterinary business is down between 25 and 30 per cent, mostly because farmers are cancelling elective surgeries for animals and skipping routine vet visits. Dr. Ted Shacklady of Okotoks, Alberta, agrees with this figure. His cattle practice has declined 25 per cent since the beginning of the crisis. He does, however, find that his sale of drugs to farmers has remained strong, indicating that the farmers are taking over some of the vaccination and other drug programs previously done by the local vet.

One of the government programs put into place to help beef ranchers and farmers is the National BSE Surveillance Reimbursement Program. This program pays $75 (the Alberta government tops this up to $225) to ranchers who get a downer animal euthanized by a veterinarian. The vet takes a brain sample and sends it for a BSE test to a lab that reports to the Canadian Food Inspection Agency. Veterinarians receive $100 for these services. While ranchers were initially apprehensive about getting their animals tested, Dr. Shacklady has found that the program is now gaining customers. This program has added some income to the practices of large-animal veterinarians. While it has taken up some of the slack, it is a limited program and cannot come close to making up for lost revenues. Veterinarians have also seen a downside to the program. Some Alberta ranchers have attempted to use it to get rid of their cull animals. With no market for culls, a few ranchers, hoping to recoup at least $225, have asked vets to euthanize these animals. While sympathetic to the plight of their clients, veterinarians have resisted the temptation. Many veterinarians, like Ted Shacklady, are filling the gap in their lost large-animal revenues by treating small animals.

Like veterinarians, farm implement dealers have also suffered income losses because of customers' lack of cash flow. Hardest hit are sales of used equipment, although new sales are slumping as well. Smaller beef operators usually purchase used equipment, and today they don't have enough income to buy. Many of the larger operations can still afford new equipment because their size can offset lower beef prices. These outfits however, are in the minority, which leave new implement dealers taking their lumps along with everyone else in the beef business.

Grain prices are also down. Mixed farmers cannot make up their losses on beef by selling their canola, and that means they won't be purchasing any new or used equipment. Even the car dealers in rural areas are feeling the pinch as ranchers try to make their pickup trucks and family sedans last until better times.

The pet food industry is another sector of the economy feeling indirect impacts from BSE. Even before the first Canadian case appeared, the U.S. banned pet food containing meat from any country at risk for BSE. This ban includes dry and canned pet foods made from meat that might contain the BSE agent. Canadian pet food companies were forced immediately to stop exporting pet foods to the U.S.; any pet food already exported but not yet sold was destroyed. Pet food companies lost the revenues from these stocks, as well as from any further business with the U.S. This ban remains in place despite the fact that no dogs or cats have yet been found with any form of BSE in North America. There has been a feline form of the spongiform encephalopathy found in the U.K., so the U.S. ban may not be a totally unreasonable precaution.

Between 85 and 90 per cent of pet food sold in Canada is manufactured by large multinationals, most from the U.S. Canada has some 17 pet food manufacturers, mainly concentrated in Ontario. One Canadian pet food manufacturer that used to do business with the U.S. was Rollover Premium Pet Food Company of High River, Alberta. According to its president, Wayne Skogman, the company lost about 15 per cent of its business, amounting to about $890,000 a year, when the U.S. border closed. The company had just reorganized and was poised to make a major breakthrough into the American market when Canada got its first case of BSE. Rollover now does business with Japan and Korea, but these exports have not yet replaced those lost in the U.S.

Because the American and Canadian beef business is so integrated, the U.S. bans and closed border have created an economic backlash for some of its own industries involved in the cattle trade. Meat packing plants in the

Pacific Northwest have felt the greatest impact. Almost 15,000 head of Canadian cattle were crossing the border each week in the pre-BSE days. The abrupt end of this cattle flow meant that these plants could not get enough local cattle to maintain operations. This lack of supply was a major factor in the closure of four Tyson Foods meat packing plants—one the plant in Boise, Idaho, a major benefactor of the Canadian beef export trade. With too few cattle to process, Tyson was forced to also cut back from two shifts to one in its Pasco, Washington plant.

With no Canadian cattle crossing the border, U.S. meat packers had to pay higher prices for domestic animals. Canadian cattle had been relatively cheap for American meat packers because of the low Canadian dollar. Cattle supplies from local sources were harder to come by, and more expensive, because of the lack of Canadian price competition.

The economic consequences of BSE and the beef bans have been deep and far-reaching. They have been nothing short of a disaster for the Canadian beef industry. The good news is that the BSE crisis has uncovered fundamental flaws and weaknesses in the beef business that everyone in the industry now recognizes and seems determined to fix.

CHAPTER 7

What's Behind the Cattle Crisis

Some people have the wrong-headed notion that nothing could have been done to prevent BSE from making its way into Canada. Others, just as wrong-headedly, maintain that nothing could have been done to forestall the economic consequences when BSE did arrive. The facts tell a very different story. Canadian government officials delayed for far too long setting up the one safeguard that could have prevented BSE from getting a foothold in Canada's beef herd. And almost everyone in the cattle business was either missing or ignoring the warning signs of fundamental problems in the beef industry, problems that amounted to a disaster just waiting to happen.

It is difficult to understand why the Canadian government was so slow in banning cattle feed containing meat and bone meal produced from ruminant carcasses. The BSE disaster in the United Kingdom clearly demonstrated that the disease's causative agent was transmitted through cattle feed. Although scientists needed some time after this discovery to determine exactly what the BSE agent was, by July 1988, the British government took the precautionary step of instituting a ban on the use of ruminant-based meat and bone meal in all ruminant feed products. It would be an additional nine years later before similar bans were set up in Canada and the United States.

When the full force of the BSE epidemic of the early 1990's hit the U.K., responsibility for keeping track of animal health issues around the globe belonged to Canada's Ministry of Agriculture. This mandate passed to the Canadian Food Inspection Agency when it was established in 1997. It appears that the Ministry of Agriculture is at least partly to blame for BSE showing up in Alberta's cattle in 2003. Initially, Canadian officials may have been looking for more scientific evidence to substantiate the British ban, but by 1988, there was no doubt whatsoever in the minds of British investigators at the Central Veterinary Laboratory in Weybridge that BSE was being spread through cattle feed containing meat and bone meal. This was the only factor common to all the early cases. Other pieces of the BSE puzzle were still unknown. No one claimed that the feed ban was based on scientific fact, only that it was set up, along with several other measures, as a desperate attempt to halt the transmission of BSE. By 1994, there was clear evidence that the ban was working when the number of BSE cases in the U.K. began to decline. That was when the European Union, whose agricultural economy was closely tied to the British agricultural industry, also banned ruminant material in meat and bone meal.

Since there was clear scientific data as early as 1994 linking BSE to ruminant-based meat and bone meal in cattle feed, why did the Canada and the United States wait another three years before instituting the North American feed ban? The incubation period of BSE, according to a British study, averages 5.2 years. If the North American feed ban had been imposed in 1994, it seems likely that BSE would not have infected that first Black Angus in 2003. Any BSE prions in the cattle feed at that time would have caused a BSE case by the year 2000 at the latest. The extra three-year delay allowed meat from BSE-infected cattle imported from the U.K. to be processed into cattle feed for at least another four years, as indicated when a cow in Red Deer, Alberta, tested positive for BSE in 1993.

Many farmers and ranchers feel that this delay in imposing the North American feed ban was a crucial factor in Canada's BSE crisis. In April 2005 a $7 billion class-action lawsuit was filed in four provinces, Alberta, Saskatchewan, Ontario, and Quebec, against both the Canadian federal government and the Ridley Corporation, an Australia-based feed producer. These suits claim that the government lost track of 191 cows imported from Britain, cattle that should have been tracked for signs of BSE, a precaution to prevent them from being used in cattle food. The suits also claim that the Ridley Corporation should have stopped using cattle parts in its production of Canadian cattle feed in 1996, the same year Ridley ceased using cattle parts in Australian cattle feed. On June 23, 2005, the first case conference was held in the Ontario class action (covering cattle producers in Ontario, British Columbia, Manitoba, New Brunswick, Nova Scotia, Newfoundland, and Prince Edward Island). Regional Senior Justice Warren Winkler, in charge of the action right up to trial, decided that all defendants will be given the opportunity in Fall 2005 to challenge the legal adequacy of the statement of claim to decide whether the claim reveals a cause of action in the law against each of the defendants. This is the first step in any test for certification as a class action suit, and the results of this motion will be critical in determining whether the lawsuits move forward.

◆◆◆◆◆

The discovery of BSE in Marwyn Peaster's cow in May 2003 has turned out to be the catalyst for Canada's current cattle crisis—a crisis waiting to happen. For years, many people in the beef industry have been warning producers that there were too many cattle in the country and too many Canadian cattle heading to the U.S. There were also protectionist rumblings from American producers that the Canadian beef industry either missed or ignored—until it was too late.

The Canadian cattle herd has been expanding for the last 18 years. In 1987, it was about 8.5 per cent of the

American herd. By 2005 that figure sat above 13.5 per cent. In hard numbers, the Canadian herd expanded from 3.1 million head in 1987 to over 15.1 million in 2005. As Canada added more and more cows to its herd, the number of feeder calves increased proportionally. Canada was producing more beef and exporting more cattle to the U.S.

The expansion of the Canadian cow herd was driven more by the price of quality feed than it was by a perceived need for more product. In 1979, the U.S., frustrated with the subsidization policies of the Europeans, instigated retaliation policies that subsidized its own grain destined for export markets. (In the trade, these are commonly referred to as "export enhancement programs.") The competition forced down worldwide prices for grain, which in turn made it difficult for Canada to compete in export markets. When this situation was combined with the gradual removal of Crow Rate subsidies on the transportation of grain, it made the domestic use of these grains for cattle feed cheaper than ever before. Suddenly it was again affordable for ranchers to raise large cattle herds, especially in western Canada. Simultaneously, it was more profitable for U.S. farmers to raise grain, so American livestock herds did not expand significantly.

Well before Alberta had its first case of BSE, American cattle producers had begun to notice the increasing numbers of Canadian beef, both live and butchered, flowing south across their border. In 1996

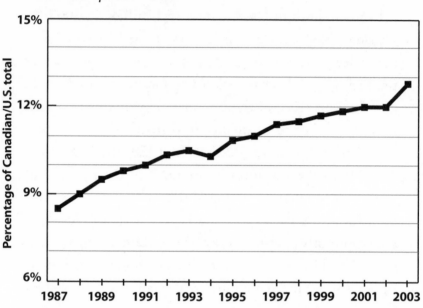

Canadian Cow Herd as Percentage of Canadian/U.S. Total

and 1997, U.S. ranchers, especially those in the northwest, believed that U.S. meat packers had begun using Canadian cattle to depress the prices paid for American animals. American ranchers have no more love for these oligopolies than do their Canadian counterparts, but they had a good point. The very low Canadian dollar was a big attraction. Because packers paid significantly less for Canadian cattle, there was no need to pay higher prices for local cattle, and they didn't. There were certainly no complaints from beef producers north of the border, who were selling lots of cattle and getting paid in American dollars.

This situation didn't sit well with some American beef producers. In 1997, Dennis McDonald, a Montana rancher, set off on a trip across the U.S. to organize support for an antidumping trade case against Canada (and Mexico). In order to file a suit with the U.S. International Trade Commission (ITC), he needed the support of 25 per cent of the American cattle industry. He got that support within three months by signing up 27,000 individual beef producers and 126 cattle organizations. R-CALF USA was born. Its suit was filed in 1998, and R-CALF was able to show that Canada was selling live cattle below the cost of production (dumping). The ITC ruled that, since the Canadian market penetration into the U.S. was "de minimus," or too small to be a significant factor, the American cattle industry was not being seriously affected. R-CALF won the case, but lost the battle. No anti-dumping duties were imposed on Canada.

After the ITC's decision, R-CALF membership declined, but the organization did not wither and die. It changed shape and became a membership-based organization representing the interests of independent ranchers. That amounted to a direct challenge to the more moderate National Cattlemen's Beef Association, the major beef organization in the U.S. In its new incarnation, R-CALF moved from anti-dumping suits, which had failed to stop the importation of live cattle from Canada, to advocating Country-of-Origin-Labeling (COOL) for all beef, from live cattle imported for slaughter to boxed beef. This legislation would mean that each beef package in the supermarket would carry labels indicating where the meat originated. The hope was that American consumers would buy American-produced beef.

R-CALF was not the only advocate of this legislation, but their lobby helped to pass COOL, and on May 13, 2002, President Bush signed into law the Farm Security and Rural Investment Act of 2002, more commonly known as the 2002 Farm Bill. One section requires country-of-origin-labelling (COOL) for beef, lamb, pork, fish, perishable agricultural commodities, and peanuts. In January 2004, President Bush signed Public Law 108-199, which postponed the implementation of mandatory COOL for all commodities covered in the act (with the exception of wild and farm-raised fish and shellfish,) until September 30, 2006. At the very least, it seems that the American meat packers lobby has been effective in delaying the implementation of this legislation. Perhaps Canadian lobbyists, like the Canadian Cattlemen's Association and the federal Ministry of Agriculture, have also played a role in COOL's delay.

Little wonder, then, that R-CALF reacted to the news of a Canadian BSE case by further promoting their protectionist cause. That meat packing plants in the northern U.S. were reducing shifts and laying off employees had little effect on R-CALF members. In their view, the larger meat packers were price-fixers, and thus the enemy. Nor did it seem to bother R-CALF that their protectionist stance may have caused the bankruptcy of Iowa Quality Beef, a producer-owned co-operative meat packing plant that opened to great fanfare in July 2003 but went broke because of high cattle costs. Iowa Quality Beef was not a member of the three major American beef processing companies—Cargill, Tyson, or Con-Agra, but it was organized by the producers themselves to facilitate the processing of some 1,200 head of cattle per day.

R-CALF took its first action against Canadian beef in April 2004, right after the USDA had announced that it would allow all edible bovine meat products into the country, including bone-in cuts, ground beef, and processed meat. This was in addition to USDA's decision in August 2003 to allow boneless boxed beef into the U.S. R-CALF immediately filed an injunction, and rather than fight this action in court, the USDA reached an agreement with R-CALF: no new meat products would be allowed to cross the border. The injunction would stay in place until the USDA produced definitive final rules covering the importation of Canadian beef products.

This final ruling came on December 29, 2004, when the U.S. announced that, on March 7, 2005, the border would reopen to live Canadian cattle and bison under 30 months of age and destined for immediate slaughter. The ruling also allowed imports of beef products from cattle over 30 months. This meant virtually a full reopening of the border to both live animals and all meat products. It is unlikely that the discovery of two new cases of BSE in Alberta, on January 2 and January 11, 2005, had any effect on R-CALF's plans. It had already announced that it would challenge the USDA's decision. However, these new cases may have influenced Judge Richard Cebull, who granted R-CALF a temporary injunction in Billings, Montana, on March 2, 2005.

R-CALF's protectionist platform was established well before Canada's first case of BSE appeared in 2003. BSE has simply given R-CALF another route to follow in its attempts to stop Canadian live cattle from crossing the border. The association has resorted to fear-mongering tactics by claiming that Canadian cattle are a danger to human health. There is no scientific evidence that BSE is anything more than a bovine disease which strikes only sporadically, particularly when the proper safeguards are in place. North American bans on using ruminant carcasses and Specified Risk Materials in animal and human food virtually eliminate any risk of contracting the variant form of Creutzfeld-Jacob Disease from eating beef.

When the first case of vCJD appeared in 1995, scientists had a tough time predicting how many people might end up dying from the disease. Figures ranged from a few hundred cases to an epidemic killing millions. By June 2005, some 150 cases of vCJD had been reported to the CJD Surveillance Unit in Edinburgh, Scotland. These included 42 cases which could not be specifically verified because no neuropathological confirmation (brain sample tests) had been obtained. In 2000, there were 28 cases of vCJD reported to the surveillance unit. Worldwide, there have been only 161 reported cases of vCJD, a figure that includes the U.K. numbers. Considering that there have been almost 175,000 cases of BSE in the British cattle herd, this seems to be a very small number of vCJD incidents. We have noted that the U.K. set up safeguards even before all the scientific evidence was in, beginning with the ban on Specified Bovine Offal. These measures appeared to be effective, as the number of vCJD cases peaked in 2000, dropped to just nine new cases in 2004, with only two in the first half of 2005. Only two cases of vCJD have appeared in North America, both victims had spent long periods in the U.K. during the BSE crisis.

To put things in perspective, the U.K. has had approximately one case of vCJD for every 1,167 cows affected with BSE. At that rate, it is unlikely that Canada or the U.S., with their ruminant feed bans and strict prohibitions against Specified Risk Material in human food, will ever see another case of vCJD. R-CALF's claims that American consumers run the risk of contracting vCJD from eating Canadian beef is nothing more than a smokescreen for a protectionist agenda.

Two other related factors, along with the rapid increase in the Canadian cow herd, turned the discovery of BSE in 2003 from an anomaly into a disaster: the declining Canadian consumption of beef on a per capita basis, and rising exports of beef and live animals to the

"The Americans have managed to turn the whole health issue into a straight case of protectionism, ignoring the fact that BSE is now about as big a safety concern as being bitten by a rabid moose in downtown Los Angeles."

Chris Mills, Canadagriculture Online, 08/23/04

U.S. These factors moved Canada from being basically self-sufficient in beef production, to being the world's third largest beef-exporting nation. On the surface, Canada's export position seems very positive, as nothing is better for any economy than a positive trade balance. This would indeed be the case if BSE had not caused the U.S. border to close.

For almost 20 years, Canadian beef consumption has been dropping. Health gurus have trumpeted the negative effects of red meat in diets, mainly because of saturated fats and cholesterol. Canadian consumers have obviously been listening. Since 1987, Canadian per capita beef consumption in Canada has fallen by 33 per cent. Figures from several sources, including Statistics Canada, Canfax, and the BMO Financial Group, show that each Canadian ate approximately 25 kilograms (55 pounds) of beef (retail weight) in 1987; that figure now stands at just over 20 kilograms (45 pounds). The rapid decline in consumption was actually much worse than these figures indicate. In 1987, when the Canadian beef herd began to expand, consumption consisted of 85 per cent domestic production and 15 per cent from imported meat. By 2002 imported beef accounted for 33 per cent of domestic consumption.

This declining consumption, exacerbated by rising imports, meant that an increasing proportion of Canadian beef and cattle production had to be exported in order for the industry to survive. In 2002 the Canadian beef industry exported 60 per cent of its production, a colossal increase from the 1987 figure of 5.6 per cent. Putting this into consumption figures, Canadians consumed 85 per cent of domestic beef production in 1987 but only 40 per cent in 2002, although, the Canadian population increased by 18 per cent during this time.

Retail Weight vs Carcass Weight

There are two ways of measuring consumption. The older way is called carcass weight, and this figure is always higher because it counts the waste as well as the useable beef. The more understandable way is retail weight, which just counts the useable beef cuts. The ratio between them is 69 per cent, which cashes out as a consumption of 70 pounds on a carcass or to just 48.3 pounds on a retail weight basis. Here are the exact consumption figures, according to Statistics Canada, for the two benchmark years:

Year	Carcass Weight Basis	Retail Weight Basis
1987	79.59	54.92
2002	66.14	45.64

The main instigator for increased cross-border trading of cattle and beef products was the Canada-U.S. Free Trade Agreement (CUSTA) of January 1, 1989. This agreement, a precursor to North American Free Trade Agreement (NAFTA), phased out all agricultural tariffs between the U.S. and Canada over a ten-year period, improved market access for products, and lowered the use of subsidies in both countries. Although tariffs were not necessarily a huge barrier for cattle because they were relatively low, CUSTA did open the borders for the freer movement of agricultural products. Cattle and beef products crossed the border without massive amounts of red tape.

The reduction in tariffs and regulations under CUSTA happened just after the major reduction in grain prices that led to big increases in the Canadian cattle herd. Since Canadian meat packing plants were suffering from old age and lack of capacity, cattle producers were more than happy to send their beef, especially slaughter and cull cattle, to under-utilized U.S. packing plants in Washington, Idaho, and Utah. Feedlots in the northern U.S. were also in need of feeder cattle at the time CUSTA was signed. Prices for beef were high and supplies of cattle, especially in the U.S. northwest, were tight.

The result was an ever-increasing flow of live cattle and beef products to the U.S. In 1990 Canada exported only 16 per cent of its beef production to the U.S., according to Professor Harlan Hughes of North Dakota State University. During in the 10-year span from 1987 to

1997, exports of live cattle to the U.S. increased from 300,000 a year to a peak of 1,500,000 in 1996. This huge increase in trade created tremendous prosperity in the Canadian beef industry. Even the addition of the Cargill plant in High River, Alberta, and the expansion of the Lakeside plant in Brooks did not slow the southern flow of Canadian cattle. Canada was producing enough cattle to supply domestic demands, and the unfilled needs of the American market. By 2002, 22 per cent of live animals were being exported to the States and another 27 per cent of beef products were going south, for a total of 49 per cent of Canada's beef production. Only 40 per cent of Canadian beef was consumed in Canada, while the remaining 11 per cent was exported to other countries.

In the early 1990s, American beef prices were high and the U.S. market needed cattle, but an even more important factor was at work—the decreasing value of the Canadian dollar. From a relative high in 1990 of 85.7 cents (versus the U.S. dollar) Canada's loonie slumped to 72.9 cents in 1995, and finally to a low of 62.5 cents in 2001. This made Canadian cattle and beef very cheap for American packers and feedlot operators. According to Professor Hughes, "the relatively low value of the Canadian dollar since 1996 may well have been the single largest contributor to the increased Canadian beef exports during the 1990s." While beef prices were high in the U.S., everyone on both sides of the border was happy. The situation was all too good to last.

Prices for beef in the U.S. remained high through the first few years of the 1990s, so Canadian cattle were needed to meet demands. Then feed grain prices in the U.S. began to rise, and costs of raising beef cattle rose accordingly, causing beef prices to increase. American consumers, who had been gradually decreasing their beef consumption, bought even less. As demand fell, the prices dropped, and producers were suddenly not receiving the high same prices for cattle that they had been accustomed to. Beginning in 1994 and continuing through 1996, the price slump caused value of feeder calves to drop below the value of the slaughter cattle (cull cows & bulls). The influx of cattle from north of the border thus became a burden for American ranchers.

In the early part of the 1990s, North Dakota cattle producers were making a profit of between $152 and $192 (U.S.) per cow. From 1994 to 1998, the same producers were making only $3 per cow. In two of these years, the average producer lost money.

Despite the low prices American producers were receiving, meat packers and feedlot owners continued to import cheaper Canadian cattle. In 1998, American cattle producers began blocking highways with their tractors to stop trucks bringing Canadian cattle into the country. In the fall of 1998, the governor of South Dakota went so far as to refuse entry to all trucks carrying Canadian grain, cattle, or hogs. South Dakota and other neighbouring states began pulling over trucks loaded with Canadian cattle for unnecessary inspections. By 2000, U.S. cattle prices returned to their pre-slump levels, at between $130 and $150 per cow, but by this time, R-CALF's beef producers were up in arms and waiting.

By increasing exports to the U.S. from 16 per cent of Canadian beef production in 1990 to a high of 49 per cent of a much larger number of cattle in 2002, ranchers became overly dependent on the U.S. market. And as all this exporting was going on, Canada began to import huge quantities of beef from other countries not included in the North American Free Trade Agreements (NAFTA). These exporters included Australia, New Zealand, and Uruguay, a clear indication of just how out of balance the beef industry was before the BSE crisis unfolded.

Initial Canadian importation of beef appears to have been the result of a trade agreement signed by Canada and other members of the World Trade Organization (WTO). The WTO provides the multilateral trade rules that govern Canada's commercial relations with its 147 other member nations. All of Canada's most significant trading partners are members, although developing countries make up the vast majority of WTO membership. Established in 1995, the WTO is the successor to the General Agreement on Tariffs and Trade (GATT).

WTO's overall objective is to "increase economic growth and raise standards of living by making trade more free and predictable." The agriculture part of the overall WTO agreement was negotiated in the Uruguay Round of talks that took place from 1986 to 1994. This step was considered to be a significant first initiative toward fairer competition and a less distorted sector between developing and developed nations—between the rich and poor states of the world. It included specific commitments by WTO member governments to improve market access and reduce trade-distorting agricultural subsidies. During the Uruguay Round of talks, Canada committed to importing 76,409 tonnes of beef each year. Unfortunately for beef producers, there were no provisions requiring non-NAFTA countries to import Canadian beef in return. Why anyone should accept an agricultural commodity that the country does not need in the quest to make trade more "free and predictable" is a question that only politicians can answer.

Canada was not the only country that agreed to accept beef it did not need. The U.S. agreed to take in 696,621 tonnes. (These figures were based on the five-year average amount of imports during the late 1970s.) The story gets worse. Canada was actually importing almost 50 per cent more than it was required to under the WTO accord. By 2003 the total amount of beef imports from non-NAFTA countries amounted to an astounding 158,800 tonnes.

How did this happen? The answer appears to be that too much beef, especially lower-grade products from cull cattle, was being sent to the U.S. for slaughter and consumption. Canadian meat packers were more than happy to send their products to the U.S., because then they did not then have to meet the specifications built into the imported product. One huge customer was MacDonald's hamburger chain. Ian McKillop, president of the Ontario Cattlemen's Association, contends that Canada could not supply a consistent enough product. As a result, importers simply applied to the government for "supplementary quotas," duty-free product above the 76,409 figure, and the government readily gave it to them. Obviously, consistency was not the only factor. The price had to be equivalent or cheaper, or this complex method of satisfying consumer demand would not fly.

We are surprised to discover that it would prove cheaper to import beef all the way from Australia than to ship it from Alberta, but this seems to have been the case. When the first BSE animal was discovered in May 2003, the immediate closure of the U.S. border combined with the continued import of foreign beef created a huge glut of beef on the Canadian market. Prices that producers were able to get for their animals from the meat packers dropped, and the crisis was on.

With the exception of keen-eyed cattlemen like Charlie Gracey, past president of the Canadian Cattlemen's Association, few people in the industry, and perhaps no one in government, saw anything wrong with the supplementary quota system. When the BSE crisis hit, our reliance on imported beef returned to haunt Canada's beef producers.

The Canada Beef Export Federation made valiant efforts to seek new export markets for Canada's conventional beef products, but little was done by producers or their representative to tap entirely new domestic beef markets.

Someone should have been taking notes when early fears about growth hormones and antibiotics in beef products were reported. Most consumers are more concerned that hormone residues will cause cancer or change the way their bodies work than they are about falling prey to "superbugs" resistant to antibiotics. To date, there is no conclusive evidence that either growth hormones or antibiotics have any effect on the health of people who eat beef. Throwing science at consumers to convince them that eating beef is safe doesn't work. A more fruitful approach would be to give the customers what they want —beef that is guaranteed to be free of growth hormones and antibiotics.

There are two kinds of chemical-free beef: organic and natural. Organic indicates that no hormones or antibiotics have been ever given to the animal, and also that all administered feed has been free of pesticides. Natural indicates that no hormones or antibiotics have been routinely given to the animal. This category does allow antibiotics use to treat disease, although not as a preventative measure. Feed controls are not specified in this category.

Producing organic or natural beef is not easy, or is it cheap. Ranchers must raise organic calves on chemical-free land. Feedlots must finish them on chemical-free grain. Meat packers must slaughter and process them on kill lines not contaminated by residue from run-of-the-mill cattle. These are a few good reasons why organic and natural beef is only available in very small quantities at a relatively high price from specialized producers. Few consumers are willing to pay for these costs, thus convincing producers that there is little demand.

Nevertheless, demand would increase considerably if organic or natural beef were available in large quantities. That would require increasing domestic consumption by mass-production and mass marketing a premium product to health-conscious consumers. This is a strategy that would also open up new export markets by satisfying the European Community's demands for a hormone-free beef. That, in turn, would cut Canadian producers' dependence on the American beef. Developing new domestic and export markets is essential to ensuring that once this cattle crisis is over, another one doesn't roll in behind it.

CHAPTER 8

Crisis
Management

Why has this crisis in the cattle industry dragged on so long? There was certainly nothing the "little guys"—individual ranchers and farmers—could do to convince the U.S. government to open its border to their calves and cattle. Getting an appointment with the USDA would have been the hardest part, but even if producers had been invited in for a discussion, it wasn't their job to solve international trade problems. That was, and is, the responsibility of the federal government, provincial governments, and their cattle associations. Not only did the federal government need to solve the trade problems that ranchers and farmers were facing, it also needed to make amends. Its Canadian Food Inspection Agency had played a big part in allowing the crisis to happen.

The Canadian Food Inspection Agency (CFIA) was created in 1997 to consolidate food safety and inspection programs of four separate federal ministries: Agriculture and Agri-Food Canada, Health Canada, Fisheries and Oceans Canada, and Industry Canada all had sections whose functions overlapped, and at least four key reports between 1970 and 1985 had recommended establishing a single agency in order to co-ordinate all government food inspection programs. When it was created, CFIA inherited from the four departments 12 pieces of legislation, 46 sets of regulations, and 4,500 employees divided into 27 different bargaining units. It took several years to consolidate all these programs and regulations, and to distill the bargaining units down to a more manageable level. As CFIA was sorting all this out, its budget was cut by $33 million. Today, the department has 4,600 employees in just four bargaining units. It maintains 14 inspection programs that cover food, plant, and animals, and has divided the country into four areas with 18 regional offices. To deliver these programs, CFIA maintains 185 field offices and 408 offices in non-government establishments, such as meat packing plants. It also maintains 22 laboratories and research facilities to support these offices.

CFIA has a broad mandate to cover food safety, animal health, and plant protection. The Canadian government likes to call CFIA "Canada's food safety watchdog," and points out that "safe food begins with healthy plants and animals." According to the government, "CFIA works to prevent foreign diseases and pests from getting into Canada." In the areas of animal health and meat safety, CFIA's responsibilities include:

- monitoring more than 1,500 international agreements that cover all aspects of safe international trade in animals and foods
- monitoring animal health issues around the world
- certifying animals and animal products for export
- border inspections for foreign pests and diseases
- laboratory testing
- inspection of federally registered meat-processing facilities
- verifying the humane transportation of animals
- conducting food investigations
- issuing food product recalls
- enforcing food labelling regulations
- performing environmental assessments
- conducting risk assessments

CFIA may have performed some of its mandates as required by providing essential services in its first few years as a full-fledged agency. But it failed to protect the health of the country's cattle herd, which became obvious in May 2003, when BSE managed to slip past Canada's food safety watchdog.

In 1993, when the four federal ministries were looking after animal health issues, BSE cattle were imported into the country. After the cow in Red Deer, Alberta, tested positive for BSE, these ministries set up a program to monitor all imported cattle still alive, but then lost track of some important specimens, such as those that had come from British herds with reported cases of BSE. It is likely that a few of these animals died of BSE and that their rendered carcasses ended up as cattle feed; the chain of transmission was initiated.

It was also these ministries that took so long to draft legislation for banning ruminant material in ruminant feed. CFIA introduced such legislation in August 1997, 14 years after British scientists had established that BSE was transmitted through cattle feed and almost a decade after the U.K prohibited the use of ruminant products in cattle protein supplements. It was a good piece of legislation, but came too late. BSE was already incubating in some domestic Canadian cattle.

By then Ireland, Portugal, Switzerland, Belgium, and France had cases of the disease, and beef-exporting countries were doing BSE-risk assessments to reassure beef-importing countries that their cattle were safe. Canada's auditor general's report for 2000, advised CFIA to move on a BSE-risk assessment for Canada: "the agency needs to more comprehensively assess the risks that must be managed, decide on how much risk to accept and determine the resources it needs to deliver an appropriate program based on these risk decisions." The auditor general even told the agency how to calculate risk: risk to food safety is determined by combining the probability that a hazard to food safety will have an adverse effect with the magnitude that the effect is likely to have. The formula would be R(risk)=P(expected frequency) x C(consequences or impact). It seems that CFIA wasn't very good at following instructions. The BSE-risk assessment it released in 2003 was badly flawed; it only estimated the potential frequency or the chances that BSE might occur, and did not take into account the devastating impact that even one case would have on the country's beef industry. According to CFIA figures, the probability of BSE occurring in the Canadian cattle herd was 7.3 x 10^{-3} chances, or about 7 chances out of 1000 for the period prior to 1997. This figure took into account the number of cattle imported from the U.K. and the possibility that they entered the animal food chain when slaughtered and rendered. No such assessment was done for the period after 1997. While the probability was low, it was not zero, and if the impact of the discovery of a case of BSE had been included in the formula, the figure would have been much higher.

For example, the impact of a case of salmonella poisoning on a local restaurant would include the restaurant's closure until investigators determined the source of the infection and what new sanitary measures were required to protect human health. The restaurant would suffer at least two big losses: its income and its reputation. The impact of a single case of BSE on the Canadian cattle industry shouldn't have been too hard to figure out. Most major countries, including Canada, have guidelines to follow when a country reports a case of BSE: they immediately ban the importation of live cattle and meat from that country, a ban that can last for up to seven years. Unfortunately, CFIA did not factor impact into its BSE-risk assessment. And that made it possible for the agency to say that the chance of an animal being infected in Canada was "negligible."

The only significant action that CFIA did take was the introduction of legislation designed to prevent the contamination of human food by BSE-infected cattle. The legislation required the removal of Specified Risk Material (SRM) from animals over 30 months of age during the slaughtering process. The legislation came into effect on July 24, 2003. However, it took almost another full year before the agency developed a plan to ban SRM from all types of feed so that cattle would not be exposed to BSE by accidentally eating hog, poultry, or pet feed, which still contained that SRM from cattle, or by eating cattle feed contaminated in the manufacturing process. Finally, on December 10, 2004, the CFIA released its proposed amendments, which still have not yet been approved. Like the ruminant-to-ruminant feed ban, this action came far more slowly than it should have, because the risk of BSE was no longer negligible. The disease had already been found in Canada. As it turned out, CFIA failures proved even worse than this.

CFIA failed to follow up on the provisions of the 1997 cattle feed ban. By 1994, the British had already discovered that there were instances of sloppy compliance with the U.K.'s ban on ruminant material in cattle feed. Many new cases of BSE were appearing because contaminated feed was still being sold, or farmers were still using up old feed, manufactured before the ban, or feed mills were using poor cleansing methods, and food meant for pigs and chickens was contaminating their cattle. Apparently, the negligible risk of getting the disease in Canada prevented CFIA from heeding the British experience. Evidence surfaced repeatedly, from at least 1999 on, that Canadian feed mills were not complying with the Canadian ban. In 2000, Canada's auditor general noted that "problems exist in compliance activities," and recommended that CFIA "identify and adopt management practices that reasonably assure the achievement of its policy of timely correction with non-compliance with no recurrence." In other words, even when establishments were inspected and found with violations, CFIA was doing little to ensure that violations were corrected.

A frightening report, entitled "Risk Assessment of Transmissible Spongi-form Encephalopathies in Canada," was commissioned by Health Canada in 2000 and written by toxicologists Joan Orr and Mary Ellen Starodub. In it they stated: "The implementation of the ban on the feeding of ruminant derived MBM is largely an honor system monitored by the CFIA. Therefore, the possibility exists for an individual producer to either deliberately or accidentally feed prohibited materials to cattle, sheep/goats or captive cervids." This report was never released. Why commission a report, which is both important and costly

($236,840), if the results are not published? If writer Andrew Nikiforuk had not requested the report under the Freedom of Information Act, its contents might never have seen the light of day. Were the results too damning of CFIA and other government authorities? And why was Health Canada doing this report when the responsibility for food safety belonged to CFIA, under the Ministry of Agriculture and Agri-Food?

CFIA's negligence was exposed in 2004, seven years after the implementation on the ban of ruminant material in cattle feed, when 20 of 28 feed samples tested by the agency were found to contain animal parts. Even worse, a purebred cow from the farm of Wilhelm Vohs in Innisfail, Alberta, was found to have BSE in January 2005. The suspected cause was feed purchased in 1998, one year after the introduction of the feed ban. Apparently, this feed had been produced before the ban, but was still in stock at Vohs's local feed mill. CFIA had not recalled old, pre-ban stock of animal feed as part of the ban, perhaps because it still considered that there was a negligible risk that BSE would arrive in Canada.

The combination of the *Vancouver Sun*'s announcement about the contaminated feed samples, and the hard-on-the heels discovery of the new BSE case of case in Alberta was another nightmare for Canada's cattle industry. For R-CALF, it was a dream come true. It used the information to support its lawsuit requesting an injunction against the reopening of the border to

"Cattle producers, like most taxpayers, can no longer be counted on to believe what their leaders are saying. What the BSE issue needs is a formal enquiry into how it has not just been handled, but how it has been bungled and manipulated by all the players involved."

Will Verboven, Alberta Beef Magazine, *November 2004*

live Canadian cattle, which had been scheduled for March 7, 2005.

As journalist Andrew Nikiforuk and William Leiss pointed out, the CFIA also ignored a considerable amount of available scientific research and common sense. The Canadian government is still relying on CFIA for advice on handling of the BSE problem, instead of investigating CFIA's mistakes and effectiveness. This could be a large part of the reason why government policy itself has so far been unable to manage the crisis.

It certainly is true that the Canadian government financially supported the cattle industry throughout this crisis. There has been a bewildering array of government support programs designed to keep producers, cattle feeders, and even meat packers in business until the American border reopens. Provincial governments have also made financial contributions to these levels of financial aid.

The first program was established very shortly after the U.S. border closed. On June 18, 2003, the federal government started things off with the first of its BSE

Recovery Programs, with the contribution of $312 million to support cattle producers. Alberta added $100 million to the program for its cattle ranchers and farmers, and Ontario added $82 million for its producers. Other provinces also joined the program, including Manitoba, Saskatchewan, and even PEI. Total federal funding for the program eventually reached $520 million.

The BSE Recovery Program established a base price for cattle at slaughter, and when actual prices were below this, producers would get the difference, based on a sliding scale. For example, if the base price was $1.05 per pound, and the actual price turned out to be $.90, then government would pay 90 per cent of the difference or, in this case, $.14 per pound. If the price dropped to $.70, then producers would get only 84 per cent of the base price, bringing the total amount received to $.99 per pound. The costs of this program were shared 60:40 by the federal and provincial governments. While this program helped the producers, mainly the feedlot operators (since the cattle involved had to be on feed as of May 20, 2003), it obviously did not help much when the price temporarily dipped to just $.25 a pound immediately after the border closed. It did help a great deal, however, when prices rebounded on the reopening of the border to boxed beef, although revenues never again reached pre-BSE levels.

An unexpected result of this first program, which upset ranchers, consumers, and probably even government officials, was the huge windfall for meat packers. In throwing the BSE Recovery Program together as fast as possible, the federal government didn't seem to think things through carefully. It, along with the provincial governments and the Beef Information Centre, an organization funded by cattle producers, moved rapidly to establish a campaign promoting domestic beef consumption. The intentions were good: keeping Canadians eating beef would ensure that producers would not be hit with the double whammy of closed borders and dwindling markets at home because fear of vCJD. The campaign was successful and beef consumption rose slightly—the figure seems to be about 5 per cent, although some people don't agree that Canadians were eating that much more beef. At least consumption did not drop, and the market for beef remained firm.

However, the beef campaign's timing was off. It was out there winning the consumer challenge in the summer, just as the normal marketing season for much of the Canadian cattle herd was approaching, and there was a glut of cattle on the market. The BSE Recovery Program enhanced this glut by encouraging producers to sell while the program was in effect. Meat packers were swamped with beef, and good business people as they are, dropped their prices to producers. Since the demand for beef remained high from the consumer side, packers did not drop prices significantly to their wholesalers. By buying at very low prices and selling at normal prices, they tallied up huge profits. According to Alberta's auditor general's report in July 2004, the packers' profit during this period was $176 per head, almost four times higher than the profit of $46 per head (before corporate interest and taxes) that they were making before BSE. Given the capacity of both Cargill and Lakeside Packers at the time, about 4,000 head of cattle a day, this amounts to a bonus profit of about $520,000 each day cattle prices stayed low. The auditor general reported that profits remained at this level until the end of December 2003. During this time, meat packers slaughtered 1,118,803 head of cattle. This amounts to an obscene profit over this six-month period of $145,444,390, mainly for Cargill and Tyson Foods (owners of Lakeside Packers), but also for Canadian-owned XL Foods. These figures are only for Alberta. Other large packers, such as Better Beef in Guelph, Ontario—now owned by Cargill—and Levinoff Meats in Montreal, also made large profits.

Some of these meat packers also own cattle. While the figures for Cargill are not known, because it is a privately owned company, people in the industry claim that each of the multinational meat packers owns about 30,000 head of cattle being finished in feedlots. That meant that packers had a continuous supply of cattle to sell on the market and to slaughter at their plants. Owning cattle on feed qualified them as producers, which made them eligible for financial support under the government's initial BSE Recovery Program. It's hard to imagine a better situation for these already very profitable companies: making massive profits on the difference between the buying price of the cattle and the selling price to the whole-salers, while at the same time receiving federal money for their own feeder cattle.

Because of a storm of protest from both beef producers and consumers, the federal government and the government of Alberta decided to investigate the meat packers. Initially, packers refused to open their books to federal auditors. Parliament threatened to impose fines of $250,000 a day, but for reasons understood only by them, both the Conservative Party and the Bloc Quebecois voted against this legislation. The federal election campaign ended any further action in this area.

The auditor general of Alberta, Fred Dunn, also reviewed the meat packing business, and concluded that its managers were only being good businessmen. So, while ranchers were going broke, packers were making profits of hundreds of millions of dollars. Estimates of the total meat packer premium from the governments' BSE Recovery Program and their excess profits range up to $1.6 billion. While this seems high, there is no doubt that huge profits were being made, most of which went back to the parent companies in the U.S.

These investigations seemed to be only token reviews, which suggests that multinational meat packers have tremendous clout with all levels of Canadian government. It's not surprising that beef producers were left wondering who their legislators were really representing.

The federal government, with benefit of hindsight, now refers to its next initiative as "Phase 2" of the BSE Recovery Program, even though law makers never seemed to have had a long-range plan in mind. Everyone in government circles apparently expected that the BSE crisis would end within a few weeks, but as it dragged on, new relief systems were cobbled together. The Cull Animal Program was announced on November 21, 2003, the Federal government committed $120 million in base funding over two years, offering to share this program with provincial governments. The program offered to pay producers $320 per animal at slaughter.

Most provinces chose not to buy into a 40 per cent share of this initiative but offered programs of their own. Alberta, for example, recognized that getting cull animals slaughtered would be a problem, so they designed the Alberta Mature Market Animal Transition Program, a $60 million program offering producers either an upfront payment if they kept the animal, or a market differential payment if they slaughtered it. Ontario included the Cull Animal Strategy, a fund of about $10 million. While the total of these two programs did not match the $700 to $800 that ranchers were previously getting for their unwanted older animals, it was considerably better than the $100 they would receive if they could find someone to slaughter their cattle.

"Phase 3" of the federal program was introduced on September 10, 2004. Called "Repositioning the Livestock

Industry Strategy," it consisted of three programs valued at a total of $378.7 million to be disbursed over two years. The first two programs were similar and included the Fed Cattle Set-Aside Program and the Feeder Cattle Set-Aside Program. The total value of these two programs was $296.3 million. The object was to keep cattle ready for slaughter (fed cattle), and those being fattened up for slaughter (feeder cattle), off the market for at least 90 days.

A somewhat strange procedure, called a reverse auction, was adopted for the Fed Cattle Program. Cattle producers called a central number to submit their bids, which included the price of the per-day assistance for feed and other factors they were willing to accept. A government committee decided in advance how many cattle it would take each week. Presumably, ranchers making the lowest bids won the auction. Once the government's quota of cattle was reached, the bidding ended, and the bid-winning cattle were tagged with the new RFID identification tags, and could not be marketed for the next 90 days. The Feeder Cattle Program was much simpler. It involved a payment of $200 per head on a percentage of the producer's inventory, with a limited number of animals eligible per province. Again, the animals had to be tagged and kept off the market until released by the program.

The third part of Phase 3 was the Managing Older Animals Program. Valued at $82.4 million, it was a set-aside program for cows and bulls that would normally have been culled. It really just topped-up the previous cull animal program.

Provinces were also invited to participate in this three-pronged initiative, but again most declined the opportunity and chose instead to offer their own assistance. Alberta, in fact, added around $127 million to the Fed Cattle and Feeder Cattle programs.

In September 2004, the Canadian government added a financial incentive to its BSE Surveillance Program, at least partly because it had committed to testing more animals in an effort to reassuring Canada's trading partners. Beef producers would be compensated for submitting their downers, or any other cattle showing possible BSE symptoms, for testing. The program offered to pay the rancher $75 for each animal; the veterinarian who euthanized the animal and submitted its brain stem to a CFIA lab for testing received $100. The Alberta government topped up these payments up with an extra $150 for the producer, paid all of the expenses incurred by the veterinarian, and paid the abattoir $75 to store the carcass and to eventually dispose of it. Ontario did not participate in this program.

As another part of the Livestock Repositioning Program, a $66.2 million Loan Loss Reserve Program, was established to help increase slaughter capacity in Canada. This program was designed to support the provision of debt capital "to all but the largest slaughter facilities." In other words, a reserve fund was established to compensate lenders if they advanced money either to build new plants, or to expand older ones. And to speed up things up, CFIA promised to "streamline" the approval process for new plants.

It was also obvious that new export markets were needed to compensate for the loss of the American market and to reduce the Canadian beef industry's dependence on the U.S. The federal government established a $37.1 million fund of multi-purpose money. Some went to such organizations as the Canadian Beef Export Federation; some was allocated to help expand the new cattle identification system; and CFIA received money to add new technical and trade experts.

None of these programs matched the complexity of the Canadian Agricultural Income Stabilization Program (CAIS) a program established in 2003 to help producers of all agricultural products. CAIS was designed to replace three former farm safety net programs and to act as a companion program to crop insurance.

In March 2004 still another program was launched. This, the Transitional Industry Support Program (TISP), involved almost a billion dollars in support money. The initial part of the program offered beef producers a flat-rate payment based on the size of their herds as of December 23, 2003. Each producer was paid $80 for each animal, except for mature bulls and cows. Owners of other ruminants, such as sheep, goats, bison, and elk, also received varying amounts per animal. The total amount injected into this part of the program was $630 million. This initiative ended on July 31, 2004.

Another $250 million from TISP was set aside for general transition payments. These were direct payments to cattle producers who had previously applied to the Net Income Stabilization Account, precursor to CAIS. These ranchers received payments based on their five-year average of eligible net sales. While the entire TISP program involved a very large amount of money, it was not the end of the support programs.

In March 2005, immediately after it was clear that the U.S. border would not reopen in the near future, Agriculture Minister Andy Mitchell added another $50 million to the fund to help develop more export markets. This money was awarded to the Canadian Cattlemen Association's Legacy Fund, which could draw from the fund to support marketing efforts of the Canada Beef Export Federation, the Beef Information Centre, and the Canadian Beef Breeds Council. These funds were but a drop in the bucket compared to the next program, announced in the same month.

This time another billion dollars was earmarked for agricultural support, $300 million of which was to go to beef producers, $220 million to producers of other ruminants, and the final $480 for grain and oilseed (mainly canola) farmers. Called the Farm Income Payment Program, it was again designed as a 60:40 split with the provinces. The new program was based on the Transitional Income Support Program, and farmers who participated in TISP would automatically receive a payment under the Farm Income Payment Program.

Federal Farm Support Programs

- $2.6 billion in federal, provincial, and territorial funding to assist the cattle and ruminant industry in the wake of the discovery of BSE in Canada, including a federal investment of $488 million for Canada's Repositioning the Livestock Industry Strategy

- $50 million federal contribution to the Canadian Cattlemen's Association's Legacy Fund to launch an aggressive marketing campaign to reclaim and expand markets for Canadian beef

- modifications to Canada's key agricultural business risk management program, the Canadian Agricultural Income Stabilization (CAIS) Program, allowing it pay out more than $1.2 billion in its first 15 months to producers hurt by drought, the impact of BSE, the Avian flu epidemic and the decline in many commodity prices

- an estimated $892 million in payments for the 2004 crop year under Production Insurance to help farmers deal with weather-related losses

- $930 million under the Transitional Industry Support Program to help farmers with income pressures move to new business risk management programs

- $104 million in new federal funding to expand cash advance programs to include livestock, allowing farmers to hold on to their products to avoid lower prices created by market oversupply. In 2004, spring and fall cash advances made $1.2 billion available to Canadian farmers, with interest costs of over $12 million paid by the federal government

Source: Agriculture and Agri-Food Canada

Besides the provincial support given to the BSE Recovery Program and the Fed Cattle and Feeder Cattle Set-Aside programs, there were several other provincial programs available to producers. For example, by June 2004 the Alberta government had contributed $402,882,627 to cattle and other ruminant producers, and by March 2005 the Ontario government was supporting the province's 20,000 producers with programs worth $130.4 million.

These huge amounts of money certainly helped beef producers, some more than others, at least in the short run. But in the long run, the support programs were no more effective than a Band-Aid on a broken leg.

There was far less federal government action on the political front, and this is where things really needed to happen. The cattle crisis became a political crisis, and producers depended on the Canadian government, led by officials in the Ministry of Agriculture, to make serious headway in the negotiations to have the U.S. border reopened to live Canadian cattle and to beef products that were more than just boneless and boxed. The Canadian government also had the responsibility of reassuring other beef-importing countries that Canadian beef was safe.

There are international guidelines to help countries assess the animal health risk of beef-exporting nations reporting cases of BSE. These guidelines govern what trade actions should be taken. These standards are set by the World Organization for Animal Health, (the English translation for Office International des Epizooties, now commonly referred to as OIE). OIE has a membership of over 160 countries. Its mandate is to develop animal health guidelines based on the available science. When the BSE crisis struck in the U.K., OIE came up with a set of criteria for assessing a country's BSE risk; this included five BSE-risk categories:

- BSE free
- provisionally free
- minimal risk
- moderate risk
- high risk

Once the first BSE case was found in Alberta, the federal government asked an OIE panel to determine what category Canada fell into, and what needed to happen to reopen trade with the countries banning Canadian cattle and beef products. The panel consisted of veterinarians and BSE experts from Switzerland, New Zealand, and the U.S. It began its investigation on June 7, 2003. The panel's recommendations led to Canada's ban on the use of Specified Risk Material in products destined for human consumption; a review of animal feed restrictions; enhanced animal tracking and tracing systems; and improved disease testing and surveillance. With these measures in place, Canada met OIE's conditions for a minimal risk country. And that determined what trade actions were legitimate.

The countries belonging to OIE have signed a trade agreement with the World Trade Organization (WTO), the international association which sets the rules of world trade. Under WTO's Sanitary and Phytosanitary Agreement, "importing countries cannot be more trade restrictive than necessary to achieve the desired national level of protection." A country's trade measures "must not be different from those applied to products within the domestic market." The minimal risk status under OIE does not restrict the trade of either live animals or meat products, except for meat and bone meal products, once the required standards for safeguarding the health of the animals and the food products have been met. Canada has met these standards, and that means American bans against Canadian cattle and beef amount to unfair trade restrictions. As soon as the OIE categorized Canada as a minimal risk country, the federal government had grounds for a trade action against the U.S. under WTO rules.

By keeping its border closed to live cattle and most beef products, the U.S. is also violating the terms of the North American Free Trade Agreement (NAFTA). Canada signed this agreement with the U.S. and Mexico in 1992, and NAFTA came into effect on January 1, 1994. The agreement's objectives include:

- eliminating barriers to trade in, and facilitate the cross-border movement of goods and services
- promoting conditions of fair competition in the free trade area

- substantially increasing investment opportunities
- providing adequate and effective protection and enforcement of intellectual property rights
- creating effective procedures for the implementation and application of the agreement, for its joint administration, and for the resolution of disputes
- establishing a framework for further trilateral, regional, and multilateral co-operation to expand and enhance the benefits of the agreement

Under NAFTA's terms, the U.S. has erected an unfair trade barrier by claiming that American cattle herds are in danger of contracting BSE if live animals are imported from Canada, despite the clear OIE standards, set by international scientists and veterinarians, that dispute this claim. Without fair competition between Canadian and

---

"It is apparent that some Member Countries are applying trade bans when an exporting country reports the presence of BSE, without consulting the recommendations in the Code or conducting a risk analysis in accordance with its OIE and WTO obligations. While the Code provides increasingly restrictive recommendations which are commensurate with the level of BSE risk in each of the country status categories, it does not recommend any other ban than the above mentioned on trade of animals or specific animal products."

Source: The OIE Standards on BSE

U.S. cattle producers, Americans producers now have their market all to themselves. Under these circumstances, the Canadian government has the right to challenge the decision of the U.S. to close its border under Chapter 20 (Institutional Arrangements and Dispute Settlement Procedures) of NAFTA and to claim compensation for lost profits under Chapter 11 (Investments) of this agreement.

After more than two years of the American border being closed, Canadian beef producers are still waiting for the Canadian government to act on either of the available options for resolving trade disputes. These actions could have been commenced as early as July 2003. There is even a fast-track provision in the NAFTA dispute resolution mechanism that guarantees resolution of the problem within 215 days. What possible reasons could there be for the Canadian government's delay?

It's not as if Canada hasn't been down this road before. Just six months into the cattle crisis, in November 2003, the Canadian Wheat Board launched a NAFTA challenge against the U.S. International Trade Commission, which had claimed that the hard red spring wheat imported from Canada was hurting the American industry. The U.S. commission then imposed a tariff of 14.15 per cent on the Canadian wheat. In June 2005, the NAFTA panel ruled the commission had failed to prove that U.S. industry was being hurt by Canadian imports. The tariff was cancelled. Clearly the system works, so why hasn't the federal government launched a similar action for the cattle industry?

In an article published in the *Farmers Independent Weekly* on September 25, 2003, agrologist Wendy Holm quotes Michael Woods, an international trade lawyer in Montreal, who maintains that using NAFTA to open the U.S. border is a "slam dunk." Woods was quoted only four months after the cattle crisis began, so at least one legal trade expert was saying that the federal government could use the NAFTA agreement to win its case against the U.S. Woods was astounded how long ranchers had put up with the lack of action. Holm replied that it was the federal government's mandate to initiate such a dispute. The Ministry of Agriculture, working with the Foreign Affairs and International Trade officials, should have commenced such action as soon as it became apparent that the border was not going to reopen within a few weeks.

So why were Canada's leaders ignoring this chance to solve the beef-trade problem? Were they afraid of the consequences of launching a NAFTA challenge for the cattle industry? Afraid of angering American business interests in Canada, such as the powerful U.S. meat packers, Cargill and Tyson Foods? Whatever reason the government had, it was keeping its secrets to itself.

While ranchers and farmers were not getting any help in setting a fire under the federal government, they were also not seeing much action from the Canadian Cattlemen's Association (CCA), the producers' own organization, getting paid to represent the cattlemen's interest in Ottawa. Founded in 1932, the CCA is a lobby organization that now represents 90,000 Canadian cattlemen in eight provinces. Only Newfoundland and Quebec cattle producers have not chosen to join this association. The CCA is funded by a "check-off" system, wherein each time an animal is sold, a check-off amount is collected. In Alberta, this amount is $3; $1 goes to the CCA and the rest goes to the provincial organization (in this case, Alberta Beef Producers). Ontario collects $2.25 per animal, and hands over $1 to CCA. Manitoba, Saskatchewan, and B.C. levy only $2 per head in total. Although this levy may not seem like much, often an animal is sold 3 times or more, and the check-off is collected each time. The total budget for the CCA is over $1.2 million per year. This money not only supports the CCA itself, but also its subsidiary branches, the Canada Beef Export Federation, the Beef Information Centre, and a research facility. The CCA has a cattleman as president and its board of directors consists of 27 cattlemen from across the country. The day-to-day operation of the CCA is handled by a permanent staff, headed by an executive vice-president, a position currently filled by Dennis Laycraft.

Dennis Laycraft claims that the CCA has "dealt well with the overall crisis" and that the federal government has the "highest level of engagement." Laycraft goes on to say that Paul Martin is "right into it" and that the finance and agriculture ministers are both "engaged." When interviewed in February 2005, Laycraft outlined the organization's three-part program, which was pulled together in August 2004: reopen markets, primarily the U.S.; creating larger domestic markets; and creating new slaughter capacity.

It is hard to credit the CCA with the increase in slaughter capacity, although the organization may have lobbied the federal government to establish the Loan Loss Reserve Program to help fund domestic meat packing plants. However, most of the increased capacity, 22 per cent in 2004 and a further 18 per cent projected for 2005, was added by the two multinational giants, Cargill and Tyson Foods—not by new domestic capacity (which may be coming within the next year or so, but is not on line yet).

The CCA certainly has not either reopened the U.S. market or significantly increased domestic consumption, although it seems to have taken one small step to address the border issue by hiring the high-priced Washington lobby firm of Blank & Rome LLP, to speak to the U.S. government on their behalf. There have been no obvious results so far.

For reasons known only to CCA insiders, the organization has walked softly without carrying any sort of stick. It consistently stayed away from any suggestion of trade action until after the March 2, 2005, court decision that kept the border closed. Then, on March 22-24, at CCA's annual general meeting, a new "action plan" was approved. The new action incorporated the three steps from the old plan, but also included steps to extend set-aside programs and expedite age-verification systems, and, finally a provision for trade action. According to CCA President Stan Eby: "We believe that initiating formal consultations under the North American Free Trade Agreement will provide a further avenue to demonstrate why resuming trade is in the U.S. best interest". This is bold language for the CCA. The problem was that months later still no trade action had been taken. CCA seemed to be waiting for the results of the July 27, 2005, court date before deciding what to do about the temporary injunction against Canadian cattle awarded to R-CALF back in March. In other words more of the "don't rock the U.S. boat" approach.

It seems that beef producers don't know what their organization is doing. One Alberta rancher and his father sat at their kitchen table and calculated how many check-offs each cow or calf went through in a lifetime. The average seemed to be three. He then asked, "Where is the $9 going?" Even Dennis Laycraft admits that CCA may not have done a good job communicating with its constituents. Perhaps because there has been so little to communicate?

Why is the CCA doing so little when it has the ability to do so much? Wendy Holm addressed that question in a *Western Producer* column on November 4, 2004. She suggested that the answer might lie with the power of the meat packers: "Because packers have the market power to punish suppliers, directors [of CCA] feeding cattle—whether on contract or as independents—can find themselves in a conflict of interest when considering positions unsupported by the packing sector." Another possibility is that CCA directors, lacking political experience, are simply under the influence of a few "entrenched Directors and staff, whose will carries the organization."

Charlie Gracey, Dennis Laycraft's predecessor as the head of the CCA, has offered another possibility: "As organizations grow, they tend to naturally be less associated with 'the cause.' Sooner or later [the leaders] treat it as a career, a profession. They don't lose a lot of sleep over things. Ultimately, in the life of an organization one can become rich enough and strong enough to turn your own resources against your own members in the sense of misleading them with good news stories. They have to do it to justify funding for this and funding for that." In order to gather funding for various pet projects, like research to lower the emission of greenhouse gases produced by cattle (which Charlie calls the "fart factor"), the organizational leaders may be selling out the beef producers who pay them.

Federal politicians in Ottawa are saying that they have not pursued trade actions because CCA hasn't asked them to follow this road. Never mind that politicians shouldn't have to be asked to do their job. CCA has the responsibility of prodding the federal government on behalf of its members, but so far it seems as if CCA has left Canadian beef producers stranded, continuing to try and subsist on government support programs. Many farmers and ranchers are falling behind in their mortgage payments. Some have already hit the stage of last resort, and sold the family farms to large corporations and wealthy oilmen.

CHAPTER 9

Into the Future

The Black Angus cow from Wanham, Alberta, was the most famous animal in the country in 2003, and its notoriety won't be forgotten in the province's ranching history. As Canada's first domestic case of BSE, it opened a window on the country's cattle industry and exposed its flaws.

Free trade agreements, starting in 1989, brought integration to the North American cattle industry, especially between Canada and the United States. And that brought 14 years of prosperity to Canadian beef producers. They increased their herds to feed the huge American market opened up to them, and shipped most of their live cattle to meat packing plants across the border. When BSE shut ranchers and farmers out of the American market, it was suddenly clear that their integration with the U.S cattle industry had created dependence and costly problems that would take years to fix.

The first major problem the Canadian cattle industry faced after May 20, 2003, was how to slaughter the more than one million cattle per year that had been being killed in the U.S. Once the border closed to these cattle, the problem of "hook space" became acute, especially for the over 30-month cull cows and bulls. Suddenly everyone in the industry was scrambling to expand existing plants and to build new ones. There is now a large assortment of plans in various stages of development.

Building Canadian Slaughter Capacity

The large number of projects planned and in the works to create domestic slaughter capacity attests to the demand and the urgency.

Province Stage	Project	Capacity	Development Stage
B.C.	Blue Mountain Packers, Salmon Arm	250 head/ day	At 40-50 /day
B.C.	Peace Country , Tender Beef Co-op Dawson Creek	1,000 head/ week	Construction started April 2005
Alberta	Cargill Foods, High River	5,000 head/ day	At 4,500/day; construction to finish Fall 2005
Alberta	Lakeside Packers, Brooks	5.000 head/ day	At over 4,000/day; construction to finish fall 2005
Alberta	Ranchers Beef, Calgary	Not Announced	Construction started; may begin operating fall 2005

Province Stage	Project	Capacity	Development Stage
Alberta	Rancher's Own Meat Processors, Edmonton	800 head/ day	Still raising capital
Alberta	TK Ranch Natural Beef, Hanna	300 head/ week	Construction to start fall 2005
Alberta	Northwest Cattlemen's Alliance, Lethbridge	1,500 head/ day	Still raising capital
Alberta	Southwest Alberta Packers, Pincher Creek	250 head/ day	Still raising capital
Alberta	Prairie Prime Processing Co-op, Beaver County	500 head/ day	Still in planning stage
Alberta	Alberta Value-Chain Co-op	100 head/ day	Still raising capital
Alberta	Canada Farm Direct	Plans to buy existing plant	Negotiating
Saskatchewan	Natural Valley Farms, Neudork/Wolseley	1,200 head/ week	At 240/day in temporary facility
Saskatchewan	Beef Initiative Group	1,500 head/ day	Still in planning stage
Saskatchewan	DMB Food Processors, Qu'Appelle	8,000 head/ week	Planning stage
Saskatchewan	XL Beef, Moose Jaw	8,500 head/ week	In operation

Province Stage	Project	Capacity	Development Stage
Manitoba	Rancher's Choice Co-op, Dauphin	1,300 head/ week	Purchasing an existing U.S. plant to move
Manitoba	Natural Prairie Beef Inc., Neepawa	1,000 head/ week	Still raising capital
Ontario	Gencor Foods, Kitchener	1,500 head/ week	At 800/week
Quebec	Colbex/Levinoff, St. Cyril-de-Wendover	5,200 head/ week	At 400/week
P.E.I.	Atlantic Beef Products, Borden	500 head/ week	Started December 2004

Most of these projects are not even close to beginning operations, and many may never get there. The history of producer-owned slaughter plants, which most of these plans involve, is not particularly good. Ted Schroeder of Kansas State University produced a report for the Canadian beef industry that indicates that the success ratio, at best, seems to be around 50 per cent. Though all the projects now in the works may not see much success, by the end of 2004, slaughter capacity in Canada had increased—from 77,000 cattle per day to 86,000. By the fall of 2005 this figure will have risen substantially. There are still, however, several problems yet to solve.

The first is that the expansion of slaughter capacity hasn't yet been able to handle cull animals. The very large plants that are already operating, specifically Cargill and Tyson (Lakeside), do not handle cull cattle. Only smaller operations, such as XL Beef in Calgary, Better Beef in Guelph, Ontario, and Levinoff in Quebec are set up to handle these older animals. Most of the expansion plans for plants to handle culls are still highly speculative and may never happen. Many people involved in these plans and expansions are finding their efforts to raise money, and get environmental approval, often frustrated, or at least delayed, by provincial governments.

To reach the goal of obtaining self-sufficiency in meat packing, facilities to kill cull cattle must be built. Governments need to support these initiatives wherever possible, especially in areas such as Saskatchewan and Manitoba, areas that presently do not have any capacity. This is the goal Canada's Loan Loss Reserve Program was established to meet. Feasible proposals need to be fast-tracked as major priorities of the federal Ministry of Agriculture and Agri-Food, and the provincial agriculture ministries.

Even if more meat packing capacity does come on line, it does not mean that the new facilities will survive. The huge multinational corporations presently dominating this industry have the economic clout to drive their competitors out of business. Both Cargill and Tyson Foods could drop their prices to consumers well below a level that any upstart competitor could afford.

Portrait of a Beef Rebel

Before May 20, 2003, Cam Ostercamp was a pretty typical Alberta farmer. He ran a mixed operation that included about 100 beef cows producing calves each year. While he never liked the kind of control that the multinational meat packers exerted on the Alberta cattle industry, he worked within the system to make a living from his grain and beef.

This all changed when the border closed, and Cargill and Tyson suddenly began making whopping profits because of their almost total control of the meat packing industry. Suddenly Cam became a rebel. Recognizing the need to add more slaughter capacity, he helped form an organization called the Beef Initiative Group (BIG). Then he set off across the country to try to raise money to build a producer-owned packing plant.

Despite two years of very hard work, Ostercamp has still not realized his dream of protecting the farming industry's small operators. In his no-nonsense language, he compares the task of raising money to build plants that will have to compete with some of the major meat packers as "trying to push shit up a river." He would much rather go back to his own farm than take on such a Herculean task, but he believes this step toward independence is too important to give up. He's right.

Canada also needs to end its reliance on U.S. meat packers as a hedge against future protectionist action from organizations like R-CALF. Getting new Canadian facilities able to operate competitively won't be enough; new operators will need some form of protection. This could take the form of government use of a Restrictive Trade

Practices Commission, which was at least partly effective in 1959-1961, enforcing the Combines Investigation Act, and keeping competition at fair levels. It cannot be assumed that the multinationals are going to take any competition in stride.

In order to protect the domestic meat packing industry, governments also have the option of giving particular financial support to plants that are not in direct competition with the big guys. This means that meat packing plants for the cull cattle and niche markets, such as organic and natural beef, could receive priority funding. Cargill and Tyson are presently only slaughtering fed cattle, as a result of new U.S. rules stating that packers cannot slaughter both under-30-month and over-30-month cattle in the same facility. While this rule has been challenged, the R-CALF injunction has kept Canadian meat packing plants from adding the slaughter of cull cattle to their businesses. Since the niche and cull cattle markets should be a priority anyway, especially because of the glut of these older animals on farms, and the present lack of domestic facilities to slaughter them, this alternative would not tread on the multinationals, and it certainly may be a more acceptable plan for a government that is not used to standing up to its neighbours across the border.

Even if Canada were able to get the slaughter capacity it needs to become self-sufficient, the cattle industry still has another big problem to solve. Beef from the 1.2 million cattle that used to be slaughtered in the U.S. will have to be sold from Canada. That requires increasing export and domestic markets.

The cattle industry already has an organization to help find new export markets. The Canadian Beef Export Federation (CBEF), partially funded by the Canadian Cattlemen's Association, established in 1989, is an independent non-profit organization committed to improving exports for the Canadian cattle and beef industry. Under its president, Ted Haney, the CBEF has a plan to reduce the dependency of Canadian beef producers on U.S. markets from 85 per cent of beef products and live animals (74 per cent of Canada's beef products and 95 per cent of the live animals exported) down to 50 per cent. This would involve increasing exports outside the U.S. to 500,000 tonnes by 2007, so that the total of exported beef reaches 1 million tonnes. By 2010 CBEF wants the situation to be even rosier with domestic consumption at 500,000 tonnes, the U.S. importing a similar amount, and the rest of the world taking 800,000 tonnes, for a total of 1.8 million tones of beef exported per year.

Haney realizes that his organization needs to increase exports to countries that have traded with Canada in the past, such as Mexico. This step also includes reopening trade with Japan, Indonesia, and South Korea, as well as reaching new markets, such as China. The CBEF has a good plan. But this small organization also faces several obstacles.

In order to re-establish export markets in Asia, much less increase the exports, Canada has to be able to prove that its beef is safe. The approach used so far, that the science shows that there is no danger to human or animal health, has not been working. These countries want concrete proof that the beef is safe, not just statistical evidence. While it may be clear to Canadian producers and governments that the scientific approach is a sound one, this does not matter if those in the export markets won't accept science as proof sufficient.

The Canadian beef industry may have to adopt one of the two more concrete methods that can be used to prove meat is safe: either age verification or BSE testing of every animal slaughtered. The first is already set up for use; ranchers just need to start taking advantage of it.

Scientists vary in their opinions about the age cattle can be considered BSE-free. Initially, this age was thought to be 30 months, so that the over-30 and under-30 categories have been used for Canada-U.S. purposes. The boxed beef being exported to the U.S. must come from cattle under the 30-month age limit. However, other countries use the more rigorous standard of 24 months. In fact, the World Animal Health Organization (OIE) uses this standard to determine a country's risk status. No matter which standard is used, it is reasonable for countries buying beef from Canada to demand proof that the beef came from cattle under the particular age barrier. Because of some very good planning on the part of the cattle industry, Canada already has the world's best identification system, one that can verify an animal's age at slaughter.

The Canadian Cattle Identification Agency (CCIA) was organized by cattlemen to establish a system that would enable them to trace cattle back to their herd of origin. The initial system, using bar-coded ear tags, was introduced January 1, 2001, and became mandatory for all cattle ranchers and farmers on July 1, 2002. Every tag carried a unique number that identified where the animal was born, and the seller uploaded this information to a central computer system. On July 1, 2001, all packing plants began reading these tags, transferring the information to the carcass, and maintaining that identity to the end of the kill line, where the carcass is given its final inspection and graded. All packing plants were included in the system.

Under the leadership of Julie Stitt, CCIA managed to overcome considerable producer and meat packer opposition. At the start, some producers thought that the identification system would mean there was a "big brother" watching their every move; others objected to the extra effort and expense the system might involve. There were several raucous meetings in which the CCIA tried to deal with beef producers' opposition by explaining that the identification system was being set up, not to check up on ranchers, but primarily to allow government agencies to trace as quickly as possible animals found to have a reportable disease, such as BSE, foot and mouth, bluetongue, or bovine tuberculosis. In the end, the system was established for a total cost of $4 million; 20 cents of the price of each ear tag goes to fund the CCIA.

Tracing Herds

When Julie Stitt, CCIA's administrator, was driving back from a holiday in late May 2003, she was alerted to the fact a cow had tested positive for BSE, and she was asked to track down its herd of origin. Julie was very quickly able to give the Canadian Food Inspection Agency the information it needed about the herd and about the identification of the herd-mates (cohorts) of the diseased animals. This information and data from the Livestock Information Service (branding) helped CFIA quickly locate all of the animals that had moved from the herd.

"The important thing," says Julie Stitt, "is to keep the government from taking this program over. We don't want another gun registry."

The bar-coded ear tags are being replaced by Radio Frequency Identification (RFID) tags. The identification number can be read by hand-held scanners at any point in an animal's journey from ranch to feedlot to meat packing plant. The new RFID system will be mandatory by September 1, 2006.

CCIA's system is being adapted to verify the age of animals. Breeders can register the date of birth of their animals in CCIA's database, which can then be used to verify that the beef of a particular animal is under 30 or under 24 months of age. That information could be used to assure importers that the meat doesn't carry BSE, which could make a huge difference in getting markets, especially those in Japan and South Korea, reopened to Canadian beef.

Another step that will convince these markets that Canadian beef is safe is testing every animal for BSE. Again, it's not about the science, which says this step is overkill; it's about giving customers what they want. So far meat packers and others in the cattle industry have been resisting this step, apparently because of the added costs of testing every animal. It appears that the Canada Beef Export Federation, which includes representatives of the major meat packers, may be holding CBEF President Ted Haney back from pursuing this issue.

In the old days, before May 2003, meat packers' margins were slim, and adding the extra $20 or so that would be tacked on to the carcass price for BSE testing was significant. The testing cost is dropping, which makes this option more feasible as a way of getting and keeping important export markets open. At the very least, it must be possible to set up one or more Canadian meat packing plants that can ensure markets in Asia that every animal processed is age verified and BSE tested.

There is a new BSE test just around the corner which may give the Canadian cattle industry another option for increasing its beef markets in Asia. This test is designed to be conducted on live cattle at the feedlot level, just before the animals are sent to meat packing plants. Although still in the testing stage itself, with both the European Food Commission and the Canadian Food Inspection Agency, this option could prove very important to Canadian cattlemen. If the new test shows promise, the

CFIA needs to fast-track its approval to help the cattle industry out of its crisis.

Other possible export markets require different strategies. Since 1989 the markets of the European Union have been closed to Canadian and American beef because of the use of growth hormones in cattle from both countries. Canada and the United States initiated trade action against the European Union through the World Trade Organization, and in 1996 WTO ruled that the European Union's position on the hormone use in cattle was not sufficiently justified. The European Union appealed and was given until 1999 to bring its policies in line with the recommendations of the World Trade Organization.

Despite the results of this process, Europeans have not changed their demand that all imported beef be produced without the use of growth hormones. The health and consumer protection directorate of the European Union went further along the same path, concluding that even Canadian products certified as being free of drugs and hormones might contain traces of the chemicals. The directorate used this audit in 2003 as the basis of its European Union Hormones Directive to uphold the ban, despite the findings of the World Trade Organization. In retaliation, both Canada and the United States imposed sanctions on the European Union without going through the World Trade Organization. That move has angered the Europeans, and the ban continues.

Canada follows the international standards set by Codex Alimentarius, which was established in 1963 by the World Health Organization and the Food and Agriculture Organization of the United Nations for the specific purpose of setting food standards that would promote fair trade in the food industry. That Canadian beef meets these international standards should be good enough for the European Union, but clearly it is not. In the midst of a crisis of too much beef and too few markets, the time may have arrived for the Canadian cattle industry to tailor some of its production to markets that want hormone-free beef. Easier said than done, of course, but this is an era when all options for easing the cattle crisis and preventing another should be on the table for discussion.

Codex Alimentarius

The international standards set by Codex Alimentarius encompass processed, semi-processed, and raw food. Its far-reaching provisions cover the hygienic and nutritional quality of food, including microbiological norms, food additives, pesticide and veterinary drug residues, contaminants, labelling and presentation, and methods of sampling and risk analysis. Codex has more than 170 member countries, including Canada.

According to Codex Alimentarius, it "can safely claim to be the most important international reference point in matters concerning food quality."

The past dependence on U.S. markets for Canadian beef and live cattle has led the cattle industry and governments to set a low priority on exportation to other countries. Everyone in the industry knows this emphasis must change, as it is highly unlikely Canada has seen the last of U.S. protectionism.

The Canada Beef Export Federation has big plans to expand export markets, but it needs more staff to promote and sell Canadian beef. The federation's president, Ted Haney, would like to set up an office in all potential importing countries. Ideally, the staff would include a veterinarian familiar with a country's animal health regulations to ensure that Canadian imports meet the standards.

Top Beef Exporters

- According to Canfax, at the end of 2004 Canada was tied with New Zealand and Argentina as the third-largest beef exporting country.

- Brazil and Australia were by far the largest exporters of beef.

- Australia supplies 21 per cent of the world's export market. Canada supplies 9 per cent.

- New Zealand, a country of four million people, has 10 million head of cattle. Canada's cattle herd numbers over 15 million.

At the same time that the Canada Beef Export Federation is out there finding new export markets, the Canadian government and the Canadian Cattlemen's Association need to be stronger and more determined in their negotiations to reopen the U.S. market. They were handed some help in June 2005 when a cow in Texas tested positive for BSE, and John Clifford, the U.S. Department of Agriculture's chief veterinarian, declared: "The safety of our food supply is not in question. I am very confident that our interlocking safeguards are effective."

They are the same interlocking safeguards—a ban on ruminant-based animal feed, a ban on Specified Risk Material in human food, and an enhanced BSE surveillance program—that Canada has in place, and both countries set up the same safeguards at the same time. That doesn't leave either the U.S. government or a protectionist organization like R-CALF much of a leg to stand on when they claim that Canadian cattle and beef pose a threat to human health. There's no turning back on free trade and the integration of the Canadian and American beef industries. Canada needs the U.S. market, and the U.S. needs Canada's beef.

The homefront also needs attention. When BSE hit, the Beef Information Centre, the beef producers' own promotion and marketing organization, campaigned hard to keep the confidence of Canadian beef consumers, and managed to increase consumption by just over 1.1 kilograms (2.5 pounds). That gain has been lost, and needs to

Beef Consumption

- In 1990 beef consumption in Canada stood at about 25 kilograms (54.5 pounds) per person.

- In 2002 beef consumption per person had fallen to about 22 kilograms (49 pounds).

- In 1990 chicken consumption was about 22 kilograms (48.7 pounds) per person.

- In 2002 chicken consumption per person had risen to 30 kilograms (67.2 pounds).

- Canada ranks fifth in per capita beef consumption, well behind the leaders, Argentina and the U.S.

be regained and increased, if possible. And to do that, the Beef Information Centre will require more staff and a bigger budget than it did in the days when Americans were happily gobbling up all the beef that Canada could send them.

More than ever before, the Beef Information Centre should be showing and telling Canadian consumers that homegrown beef is often healthier: it is generally leaner and tastier because it is well marbled. But there's more the organization can do. It is pretty well common knowledge among consumers that many cattle are routinely given antibiotics and growth hormones. What is not common knowledge are the product and veterinarian guidelines and the Health Canada regulations governing the administration and withdrawal requirements for these and other drugs to ensure there are no residues when the animals arrive at the meat packing plants. This is important information that Canadian consumers should know, and that the Beef Information Centre should publicize.

The Beef Information Centre also has a role in feeding consumer issues back to the industry it's working for. And one of those issues is the consistency of beef quality. Many consumers complain that the tenderness and taste vary widely from store to store.

One way of overcoming this problem, which the Beef Information Centre could promote to the industry, is to move toward developing beef brands—a move supported by at least two reports on consumer preferences. Both clearly show that consumers want beef with better consistency and taste, and both argue that creating brands will give consumers what they're looking for.

For example, meat packers or their wholesale distributors could develop product lines that tie beef quality to price and make the link obvious to consumers. For Calgary's XL Foods, this could be a product called XL Gold, which indicates the highest quality—beef that is tender because it is from younger animals and that has "abundant" marbling throughout a cut. Consumers will pay more for this brand, and they will know why. Buyers could expect to pay less for a medium-quality brand called XL Silver, and still less again for the lowest quality line called XL Bronze. Taking the mystery out of meat quality and grading standards could go a long way to restoring consumer confidence and increasing domestic beef sales.

Branding might also help develop Canada's domestic niche markets for beef. A demand for organic and natural beef exists, and while some minor attempts have been made to develop this niche, there's been no concerted effort to determine the extent of this market or how to grow it. Markets for organic and natural beef pay premium prices, and at least some producers and meat packers might take up the challenge if their industry offered more information about both production and processing issues and costs. To reassure consumers that they are getting what they pay for, a product branded "Canadian Organic," for example, would have to pass strict and clear government certification standards.

Cattle ranchers and farmers know that the BSE issue has uncovered problems at their production end of the industry. In the good times of high prices and ready markets, production efficiency and financial management plans tend to slip. Those days are over, and producers have been forced to streamline their operations and find more efficient ways of raising cattle and feeding beef. And that will help them compete in new and reopened markets.

Beef producers have always battled the weather, bank rates, the value of the dollar, diseases, and fluctuating prices, but BSE may be the final straw. They know that the future of their families, their rural communities, and their industry requires big reforms, structural changes, new ways of thinking, and strong commitments from the independent rancher in Okotoks to the new co-op meat packing plant in Dawson Creek, from the Canadian Cattlemen's Association to the federal and provincial governments.

Afterword

When I began working on this book, cattle producers in Canada were facing the worst crisis in the history of their industry. By the time the manuscript was finished, not much had changed. The United States was allowing boneless boxed beef from animals under 30 months of age to cross the border, but nothing else. Ranchers and farmers were still raising and feeding animals that had no market.

From the moment the United States closed its border to exports of Canadian cattle and beef on May 20, 2003, when one Black Angus cow tested positive for BSE, everyone knew the whole industry was in trouble. The U.S. was Canada's main export market, and its reopening was essential to the survival of all parts of the Canadian cattle industry. For more than two years, the industry was kept afloat by a combination of its domestic market, which consumes only 40 per cent of beef production, government support programs, and exports of boneless boxed beef to the U.S.

Finally, on July 15, 2005, Canada's beleaguered beef industry got some good news. The United States Court of Appeals for the Ninth Circuit struck down the temporary injunction against the Final Rule that had been announced by the United States Department of Agriculture (USDA) on December 29, 2004. The Final Rule declared Canada a minimal BSE-risk region, and that meant that live cattle under 30 months of age would be allowed to cross the border for slaughter. It also allowed sheep and goats under 12 months to cross for slaughter, along with beef meat and meat from other previously banned animals, such as deer, elk, caribou, moose, and reindeer. The "meat" that would be allowed into the U.S. was not clearly specified in the Final Rule, but it seemed to include such previously banned cuts as bone-in beef, along with meat from culled animals, such as hamburger.

The ruling of the Appeals Court gave a thorough history of the BSE dispute, and it very carefully struck down every argument of R-CALF and Judge Cebull, who were responsible for the injunction. It supported the line of reasoning made by the USDA, through its Animal and Plant Health Inspection Services (APHIS) branch, and the science that these arguments was based on.

Does that mean that the cattle crisis is over? The answer is: Not yet. Animals under 30 months of age can now be exported to the U.S. So, once again Canadian meat packers are competing for young cattle with meat packers in the northern United States. That competition will push up the prices for steers and heifers and end the meat packing monopoly in Canada. Still excluded from the American export market are cattle over 30 months of age, mostly cull cows and bulls.

The continued exclusion of cattle over 30 months of age from the U.S. market appears to be an act of American protectionism. Organizations like R-CALF may not be able to prevent the under-30-month animals from moving south, but their efforts to keep out the older animals means that U.S. producers have the markets for hamburger and processed meats all to themselves. The original Final Rule included a provision to allow all meat products, including beef products from older animals, to cross the border, but it was quietly removed—and no one seemed to notice or at least no one complained loudly enough to be heard. And, at present, no one appears to be addressing this problem, yet it is one that can't wait. The animals are aging, and producers are continuing to feed them.

U.S. protectionism will not go away. And there are recent examples of how cleverly protectionist interests can operate. Shortly after the temporary injunction was struck down by the Appeal Court, Montana Governor Brian Schweitzer announced that all Canadian cattle passing through Montana would require an examination by a veterinarian to guarantee that they are younger than 30 months, that they are not pregnant, and that they carry "CAN" brand. This is an obvious attempt to slow down the entry of Canadian cattle into the U.S. And it is an obvious warning to everyone—from grassroots producers to the federal government—that, even after the flaws in the industry are fixed, it will take considerable and constant vigilance to ensure fair trade in beef and cattle across the U.S.-Canada border.

The Cause of BSE

E arly research into the cause of the scrapie form of TSE had concluded that it was neither a bacteria nor a virus, and so the search widened for a new form of causative agent. In 1967 an article by British researcher J.S. Griffith, published in the journal *Nature*, proposed that the causative agent was a protein that could somehow replicate itself, a protein that the host animal was genetically equipped to make but which it either did not normally produce or did not make in an infectious form. That a protein could be an infectious agent was a radical idea at the time, but that didn't stop Stanley Prusiner from following it up in 1970s after one of his patients died of CJD.

By 1982 Prusiner had isolated the infectious proteins, which he called prions, and found that they grouped themselves into small slender filaments of an abnormal structure that resembled the amyloid found in the brains of scrapie-infected animals. Three years later Prusiner showed that there was a normal form of these prions in both animals and humans. (Later studies indicated that these particles may be important in protecting cells from free radicals.) Prusiner's research focused on how the normal prions turned into abnormal ones. He discovered that normal prions sometimes changed their shape, and the new shape appeared to have the ability to initiate a chain reaction that caused the conversion of other normal prions in the brain to the abnormal shape. Even worse, this new prion configuration could not be broken down by proteases, which are enzymes that eliminate unnecessary or worn out proteins (a process called apoptosis). The abnormal prions build up in the brain in the form of amyloid plaques, and in time this build up begins to kill nerve cells, resulting in tissue damage and the characteristic holes in the brain.

If the infectious particles were transmitted through food, the next mystery that researchers in the prion world needed to solve was how the infectious particle travelled to the brain after being ingested. Research had shown that it did not travel through the bloodstream, which meant that it wasn't absorbed through the stomach wall or the intestines. One theory suggests that prions move to the brain through the lymphatic system, which includes bone marrow, tonsils, spleen, thymus, and lymph nodes. According to this theory, ingested prions may be absorbed through the intestinal wall where lymphoid cells absorb the infectious particles and send them to other lymphoid sites, such as the nodes, spleen, and tonsils. The prions could replicate themselves at these sites and eventually travel to the brain. The problem with this theory is that prions have not been found in the spleen or tonsils of any animal. There is some evidence that they could be in the bone marrow, but even this is not well documented. An alternative theory comes from researchers at Case Western University in Cleveland, Ohio. They found that prions can enter the bloodstream in combination with a natural protein called ferritin, which stores iron and is in ready supply in meat. These two proteins seem to stick together so that they are not detected as individual prions in the bloodstream. This may explain how prions can cross the species barrier, as this ferritin protein is almost identical in a wide variety of species. However, there is yet no explanation of how these two proteins become separated in nerve tissue. There is still much to be learned about these particles, including what causes them to change their shape to the infectious form.

Not everyone in the scientific community has accepted the prion theory. British farmer-turned-scientist Mark Purdey has made a name for himself in the BSE world with his theory that misshapen prion particles are directly linked to organophosphate pesticides used in the treatment of warble fly. Dr. Frank Bastian, working at Tulane University in New Orleans, has proposed that the cause of BSE and other TSEs is a tiny bacteria from the spiroplasma family and that the abnormal prions are the result of TSE diseases, not the cause. His concern with the main prion theory is that so far no one has shown how the normal proteins manage to fold themselves into the infectious form and then cause others to do the same. Having found spiroplasma bacteria in the brains of CJD victims and animals with scrapie, Bastian believes that they are the cause of the folding of the prion.

Bastian's theory has been bolstered by a recent Japanese study that found a bacterium called Brucella abortus, which causes brucellosis in cattle, can interact with the prion protein on host cells. Proteins on the surface of the bacteria bind to the cellular prions, and the complex that results is engulfed into the cell where it multiplies and causes a brucellosis infection. Another product of this reaction appears to be the folding of the prions. According to Bastian, this may be exactly what the spiroplasma bacteria are doing to prions to cause them to become infectious. Since these bacteria are found in most insects, Bastian believes that insects are the vectors of these bacteria. This bacterial theory helps explain what might have caused the disease to appear apparently spontaneously and why cases are still appearing in Britain today, despite the feed ban that has been in place since 1988. It does not, however, explain why it started when it did, or why the feed ban has been so effective in reducing the number of new cases to a handful.

Index